Hooked Rug Storytelling
The Art of Heather Ritchie

Lesley Mary Close

4880 Lower Valley Road Atglen, Pennsylvania 19310

Dedication

Even though they cannot see it, this book is dedicated to all the blind and visually impaired rug-makers who Heather has taught in The Gambia through Rug Aid.

It is also dedicated to Pauline Halford, whose promising writing career was cut short by her tragically early death. Pauline's encouragement at the very earliest stage of writing this book persuaded me that it was worth continuing with the project, and I am very sad that she cannot see the result of her generous and unselfish advice.

Designed by "Sue"
Type set in Amulet/Zurich BT

ISBN: 978-0-7643-3695-9
Printed in China

Other Schiffer Books on Related Subjects:
Hooked on Rugs: Outstanding Contemporary Designs
Jessie A. Turbayne ISBN:0-7642-2502-7 $39.95
Hooked Rugs Today IV: Expect the Unexpected
Amy Oxford ISBN: 978-0-7643-3283-8 $29.99
Rug Hooking in Maine: 1838-1940
Mildred Cole Peladeau ISBN: 978-0-7643-2882-4 $39.95

Schiffer Books are available at special discounts for bulk purchases for sales promotions or premiums. Special editions, including personalized covers, corporate imprints, and excerpts can be created in large quantities for special needs. For more information contact the publisher:

Published by Schiffer Publishing Ltd.
4880 Lower Valley Road
Atglen, PA 19310
Phone: (610) 593-1777; Fax: (610) 593-2002
E-mail: Info@schifferbooks.com

For the largest selection of fine reference books on this and related subjects, please visit our web site at **www.schifferbooks.com**
We are always looking for people to write books on new and related subjects. If you have an idea for a book please contact us at the above address.

This book may be purchased from the publisher.
Include $5.00 for shipping.
Please try your bookstore first.
You may write for a free catalog.

In Europe, Schiffer books are distributed by
Bushwood Books
6 Marksbury Ave.
Kew Gardens
Surrey TW9 4JF England
Phone: 44 (0) 20 8392 8585; Fax: 44 (0) 20 8392 9876
E-mail: info@bushwoodbooks.co.uk
Website: www.bushwoodbooks.co.uk

Contents

Foreword

Heather Ritchie's wonderful, heartfelt narratives about her rugs add new depth to the world of rug-hooking and to our appreciation of her work. These great stories from her memory and heart are capable of inspiring in each of us the possibility to reach deep within ourselves, back into our lives, memories and hearts, and to create our own rugs from the depths of our being. Heather explains beautifully what she has hooked and why, and thus enables this wonderful style of rug-making to be possible for all.

Heather is one of the most talented rug-makers I know. Along with that talent she is very generous with her knowledge, her heart and her ability to give. Her eye for color is almost magical and her explanations help us to learn and, with any luck, to absorb some of this magic.

This book is important as a great learning experience, for both the aspiring and established rug-hooker. To Heather, a very grateful "Thank You" for opening up an avenue of rug-making that many of us don't see or don't explore. Because of Heather, we now have the ability to grow in rug-making and in our hearts.

Barb Carroll

Barb Carroll *Courtesy of Wayne Carroll*

acknowledgements

I could not have written this book without the help of several people. First, Heather and her husband Les: he and I are occasionally mistaken for one another in emails and other people's conversations, but never in person! Heather and Les accommodated me and my every request on countless occasions. Other helpers, in no particular order, include my long-suffering partner Michael, who gave me the space and peace to write as well as endlessly patient help when my nerves were fraying; our son Mat Connolley and daughter-in-law Kat Smith; my sister Margaret Whellams and her partner Michael Carr; and my friends Hannah Boyle, Barbara Fisher and Hilary Squires.

All of these people proof read every page. Their help has prevented embarrassing errors and provided many improvements. If anything is still wrong after their generosity in giving me all that help with the task of polishing the text, it is entirely my fault.

In addition Doug Scrafton, Secretary of The South Hylton Local History Society, provided a great deal of information which considerably enhanced the first chapter, and George Stephenson, one of the Trustees of the Ashington Group, was very helpful. If I have misinterpreted anybody's words, the errors are mine.

Unless otherwise mentioned, the author also took the photographs used in this book. The exceptions have been made clear below and in the captions. I am not aware of any other items which are subject to copyright but, if a credit has been unintentionally omitted, I will be more than happy to make amends in a future edition of this book.

Several people need to be thanked for their help:

Cathy Connolley, my partner Michael's very talented sister, created the line drawings which appear at the start of each chapter.

Heather allowed me to raid her personal archives for photos of her family and ancestors.

Laurence Ritchie, Heather's son, took the photo that inspired *Jackdaw Jeans* and the two photos that Heather combined to produce *Bearing Gifts*.

Mat Connolley, my son, took a photo of me with the sensitivity and understanding which comes from knowing that I hate being on that end of the lens. He also took photos of Sausie with his daughter (in *Guiding Light*), Jankey with Heather, and the labelled rugs (both in *Origins and identity*) when he visited The Gambia to take photos for Rug Aid cic, www.rug-aid.org

Gene Shepherd allowed me to use his photograph of Bolton Castle and to quote from his blog.

Barb Carroll wrote a generous Foreword and was very encouraging.

Wayne Carroll visited the late Bobbie True's home in Arrow Rock to take the photos of Heather's rug *The Mat-making Group*. He also provided the photo of Barb Carroll which accompanies her Foreword.

Helen Bainbridge provided the photo upon which *The Mat-making Group* was based, from the archives of the Swaledale Museum in Reeth, and she encouraged me in the task of writing.

Mick and Jane Bell were kind enough to allow me to take photographs of the "netty" (earth closet) in the garden of their home in Fremington. It was being used to store garden tools as well as providing a warm place for their two pet sheep, Lionel and Lulu, to sleep. I am grateful to the humans and the animals for allowing me to empty it, leaving the straw bedding on the floor, to take the photo which appears in *Scarcote*.

Bloomsbury, British publishers of Ben Wicks' book *No Time to Wave Goodbye*, kindly allowed me to quote from his account of the experiences of evacuees during WWII.

6 Acknowledgements

Owners of copyright images:

The South Hylton Local History Society: two postcards of the Hylton ferry

Sunderland Echo: The Hylton ferry 1936 (image reference 1536), Evacuees leaving Sunderland 1939 (image reference 338), Union Street market, Sunderland 1956 (image reference 1877)

Durham City Archives: Coxgreen ferry

The Science and Society Picture Library: Engraving of coal staithes 1773 (detail of image reference 10247698)

The Imperial War Museum: Dig for Victory poster (image IWM PST 0696)

Trustees of the Ashington Group: *Pigeon Crees* by Jimmy Floyd, 1938

The Francis Frith Collection: postcard of High Row, Reeth, 1955

Ceredigion Museum, Aberystwyth: milk churn

The Northern Echo: The Reeth Parliament (photo taken by Gavin Engelbrecht)

Nicky Rogerson: photo of Heather (used on the cover) and of Les's tools (*Good Companions*) www.nrweddingphotography.co.uk +44 7710 799 603

1
Introduction

I first met Heather Ritchie in 2001, although I had been given an introduction to her beautiful North Yorkshire home before meeting her. My partner Michael, his sister Cathy and I stayed there for two nights' bed and breakfast (B&B) that August under the care of her husband Les. Heather was away in Norway during that first visit, but she was in sole charge when we returned to Reeth in October 2001 for three nights. As soon as I found the web site advertising her B&B, with its cats, dogs, hens, ducks and, above all, rugs, I knew that I would like Heather. Walking through the front door of Greencroft and seeing color and texture everywhere simply confirmed my e-view — here was someone whose company I would enjoy.

When Heather and I finally met, it was three months later and my life had been altered by redundancy. Heather was in charge this time while Les was away at sea, and she listened patiently while I told my tales of woe. For many reasons, 2001 had been a terribly difficult year for me and Heather worked on a rug as I poured my heart out to this welcoming stranger. It was fascinating to see, in action, the art form that I had so admired during my first stay in Heather's home. The following April I finally met both of Greencroft's hosts at the same time when Michael and I returned to Swaledale for a four-night stay.

By now I was completely hooked! Those amazing rugs, that fund of stories (some hilarious, some tragic), such generosity of spirit, and what wonderful breakfasts cooked on the bright red Aga after a very restful and comfortable night's sleep. It all added up to an irresistible package and I have rarely holidayed anywhere other than Reeth since 2001. I can tell you this without fear of being crowded out of my favorite place to stay because Les and Heather stopped offering B&B accommodation in 2004.

Heather started offering B&B by accident, simply out of the kindness of her heart. She came across a young German woman who was trying to sleep in the shelter which features in Chapter 12, *The Reeth Parliament*. Reeth is an important overnight stop for people on Wainwright's famous coast-to-coast path and, at that time, offered far fewer places for walkers to stay. Heather was on her own a lot then because Les was away at sea two weeks out of four. Just before she met the German woman, Heather had been sitting alone in her three-bedroom house just a few steps away up the hill and her conscience insisted she do something to help. She invited the young woman into her home and gave her a bed and something to eat. Before very long, another walker arrived in Reeth with nowhere to stay. In the end, Heather listed her home in the guidebooks and on the web sites for the coast-to-coast walk. Eventually, offering accommodation to walkers, the vast majority of whom stayed just one night, proved to be too much work when Heather was already very busy with rug-making and was getting deeply involved in developing the work of Rug Aid cic. Heather and Les may now have given up offering B&B accommodation but, oh, how glad I am that they offered it when they did.

The story of Heather's life is, like the rugs she makes, colorful and rich in detail. She has created a series of rugs that illustrate episodes from her life and this book expands those individual stories into a sequence of biographical tales. Each of these tales also looks at a rug in detail and extracts from it information about Heather's technique and unique style of working.

These works of art are rugs (or mats, the words are interchangeable in Heather's lexicon) although very few of them have ever been placed on the ground because they are just too beautiful to walk on. All but one of the rugs shown in this book hang on walls or lie on the stairs of Heather's home and studio in Reeth, North Yorkshire. There are other rugs, instructional videos and more information about her classes and supplies on her web site, www.rugmaker. co.uk

The origins of the craft of rag rug-making are probably to be found in Scandinavia where people made bed covers from coarse fabric and strips of woollen cloth. These migrated to the floor to provide protection from bare earth, cold stone or draughty wooden floorboards. It is highly likely that the Vikings brought these textile creations with them when they invaded northern England, from the eighth to the eleventh centuries, and that local people adopted the technique to cover their similarly cold floors.

There are many regional names for the two main processes involved, including hooky and proddy, the two terms used in this book (see Chapter 11, *Reeth Village Green,* for a list of some of the other names). There are also many ways of working and this book starts by providing basic instruction in the hooky technique Heather uses so that anyone inspired by her creations can begin to make their first rug. The

more advanced information about Heather's other techniques, the materials she uses and her sources of inspiration will be of interest to people who have already started rug-making. Anyone who is already familiar with Heather's work should find the story of her life and her introduction to rug-making interesting. The stories also cover her dedication to expanding the technique into an art form and her desire to teach rug-making to people in deprived communities in Africa to help them gain an income.

The esoteric rug-making terms and the names of people, places and things which appear in these pages, as well as those British English words and expressions which may be unfamiliar to some readers, are listed and explained in the glossary.

2

Preamble: the basic hooky technique

Hooky, or hooking, is one of the two most common techniques of rag rug-making, and it is the technique Heather uses most often. Hooky can be defined as using a hook to pull a sequence of loops of fabric or yarn through a backing of open weave fabric. The other technique, proddy, is explained in Chapter 16, *Paradise Garden*, one of the few rugs in this book which features the technique.

These basic instructions assume that you are right-handed — apologies to all left-handed readers — and they also refer exclusively to a strip of fabric (rather than a length of yarn) because fabric is easier to use when you first start rug-hooking. In Heather's opinion, closely-woven pure wool flannel is the best fabric to use.

Heather finds that a strip about 14 inches (35.5cm) long is the most convenient. Regardless of the type of fabric, a longer strip can be unmanageable, although rug-makers of old would roll a long strip into a ball which they unrolled as they worked. In contrast, a much shorter strip can be perfect when you only need a few loops of one fabric.

The width of the strip is governed by many factors: ¼ inch (6mm) is a good width for a beginner to use. (For instructions on cutting your strips, see Chapter 5, *The Evacuees*.) Many of the rugs in this book use very narrow strips worked with a fine hook. The technique is exactly the same but it takes longer to cover the same area, so it is a good idea to stick to ¼ inch (6mm) strips until you have mastered the technique.

The fabric you choose has an impact on the appearance of the finished loops: flannel makes nice crisp "square" loops while yarn makes soft, undefined loops. The height of the loops is governed by the width of the strip.

The first time you use a strip, hold one end of it in your left hand underneath the backing. Push your hook through from the front, catch the strip and pull the free end up through the backing. This will create a flying end on the front of your work which you should leave about twice as long as the strip of fabric is wide, ½ inch (12mm) high if you are using a ¼ inch (6mm) wide strip.

Left to right: a flying end and a first loop on the front while Heather pushes her hook through the hessian; Heather starts to pull up the second loop; Heather pulls her hook out of the third loop she has formed.

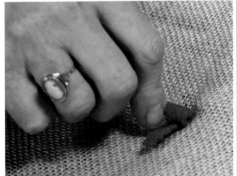
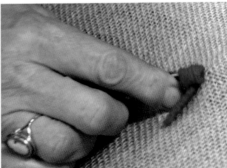

To make a loop, move your hook a few threads across the backing to the left of your flying end. A gap of two or three threads is ideal for most fabrics when you are working on a hessian backing but, as with most aspects of rug-making, Heather does not have a hard and fast rule. Make sure you hold the strip you are working on in your left hand at all times, and always hold it fairly close to the point at which it last emerged onto the back. To make a loop, push your hook down through the backing and catch the strip again. Pull the fabric through to the front of the rug, twisting your hook slightly to the right as you come up. This perfectly natural movement ensures that you are only pulling on the free end of the strip under the backing, the end which trails away to the left and is controlled by your hand. Repeat this sequence — push, catch, pull, twist — until the strip is all used up and you pull the other flying end through to the front.

When you start rug-making, pay close attention to this little twist to the right until it becomes second nature to pull only on the free end of the strip. One of the most frequently-heard complaints amongst new rug-makers is that they are pulling out their previous work when they make subsequent loops. Giving the hook this little twist to the right as you form the loop prevents this. It also keeps the pile of the rug away from the backing as you prepare to make your next hole.

It is very important to ensure that the inside of the hook end of your tool catches the far side of the strip so that you pull on the whole width of the strip as it comes up through the backing. If your hook does not pull evenly on the width of the strip, you will end up with a series of lumps of fabric on the reverse rather than the ideal series of flat short "stitches" of fabric which allow your rug to lie (or hang) completely flat.

Always take great care to push your hook into one of the holes between the threads of the backing. The backing is the weakest part of any rug and it is important to avoid splitting the fibers. Using top-quality backing fabric, such as even-weave hessian or linen, will make this easier by presenting you with a series of regularly-spaced holes for your hook to go through.

The height of the loops you make is another area where Heather does not impose rules. Her usual practice when working on a pictorial rug is to make even-sized loops about the same height as the width of the fabric strip, ¼ inch (6mm) high if you are using a strip ¼ inch (6mm) wide. That simple guide is very easy to judge by eye as you work. Many of the rugs in this book make a feature of using loops of varying widths and heights. If that appeals to you, persevere with the basic technique until you have mastered it.

Using mixed sizes of loop will be easy once you have gained plenty of experience. As you will find out in detail later in this book, longer loops can be cut to produce two flying ends in a technique called cut high loops or shearing (see Chapter 4, *Victory Garden*).

It is vital to start each new strip in the hole which contains the end of the previous one. As well as keeping the flying ends tidy, this ensures that they are held secure. They are less likely to come out of their shared hole because each one keeps the other one in place, snug and tight. The pile of loops holds the flying ends secure against being caught and pulled out and, if you trim them neatly, they will be almost invisible.

It may be that you have reached the end of the strip, or that you have simply used as much of it as is needed in a particular area of the design. Either way, you can trim the pairs of flying ends as you go, if that sort of neatness is important to you, or you can save all the trimming for later if you just want to press on. The ideal length to trim a flying end is level with (or just below) the height of the loops.

One of Heather's very few rules is that virtually no backing fabric should be visible on the reverse or front of the finished rug. It is the pile that creates your picture or pattern — the backing is less exciting

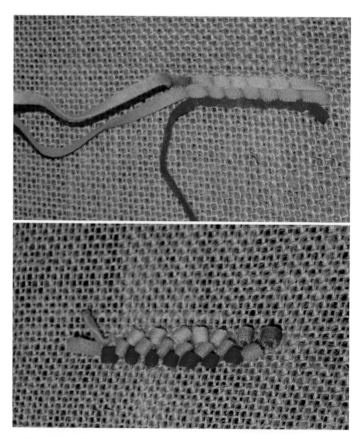

In this example of hooky, Heather has cleverly fitted three different colors of dyed flannel together – these loops are more widely spaced than her normal work to allow them to nest together.

to look at and, importantly, is much more vulnerable to wear. Covering the whole backing with pile fabric is important if a piece of work is to resist wear, whether it is destined to lie on the floor or to hang on the wall.

Taking care over the spacing of individual loops and rows of hooking will ensure that you cover as much of the backing as possible. Parallel rows should be quite closely spaced, depending on the thickness of the pile fabric you are using. Heather leaves just a thread or two of backing between rows when using flannel or sweaters. If you are using directional hooking, simply follow the direction of the previous row of loops and work a thread or two away from them wherever possible.

It is important not to put a loop in every hole of your backing. This will pack in too much fabric and put the backing under strain. That tension will break the threads, weakening your rug, and the backing is also likely to bulge and prevent it lying flat. Your work must lie flat because bulges will detract from the design if your rug hangs on the wall and, on the floor, bulges will present a danger to anyone walking on the rug. You have to achieve a happy medium and the best way to do this it to keep an eye on the tension as you work, remembering to leave spaces every so often to give your work room to breathe.

One more of Heather's very few absolute rules is, "if ever you are tempted to work in the opposite direction, don't do it!" Once the basic technique feels natural to you, working backwards will feel awkward. This is partly because, with your body in a good position for rug-making, your arm does not rotate inwards as far as it rotates outwards, so changing the direction of your twist while keeping it effective is almost impossible. It is also very slow trying to work with the trailing end of the strip on the wrong side of your completed loops. Unless you are one of those very rare people who is truly and comfortably ambidextrous, the solution is simply to turn the work around in your hands until you can work right to left again (or left to right, if you are a left-handed rug-maker). It is very easy to work all designs this way, even complex pictorials, and it is much quicker to flip the work around every so often to check your progress than to try working backwards.

Once you have mastered the basic technique, hooky rug-making is a fun and quick way to create beautiful, unique and lasting works of art. The tips Heather passes on in this book will help you to take your technique beyond the basics and her beautiful rugs will encourage you to develop your own style.

Let's be Friends: made for an exhibition (The Nest) in 2008 and included "just for a bit of fun" (as Heather often says), this rug is a real mixture of cuts, techniques and textiles. It features a needled felted bee and more than one mouse, real twigs for the besom which has caught up some dyed Swaledale fleece, knitted leaves, and a sparkling spider's web. 24 x 36 inches (60 x 91cm), mixed fabrics on a linen backing. *Collection of the artist.*

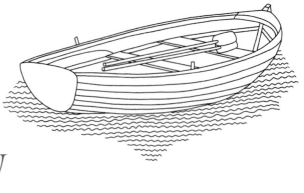

3

The Ha'penny Ferry

The Hylton Ferry, 1936. *Courtesy of Sunderland Echo*

Bessie Robson and her mother. *Archives of the artist.*

Like virtually all of the rugs in this book, *The Ha'penny Ferry* is a memory rug. As with many of the other rugs Heather has created, it is a record of something which has played an important role in shaping her life. The design of this rug reflects a photograph held in the archives of the *Sunderland Echo* showing the ferry at Hylton on the River Wear in north east England. This photo was taken in 1936 when the ferry was operated by Mr. Glasper. Heather chose to make a rug based on this image to celebrate her ancestors' many connections with water, some of which are explored further in Chapter 18, *Origins and Identity*.

Heather's paternal grandfather, William Robson, was born at Winlaton, south west of Newcastle on the River Tyne, in 1861. In 1882 he married Elizabeth Elliott who was four years older than him. Like her father and grandfather before her, Elizabeth was born at Coxgreen, about two miles (3.2 km) upstream from Hylton.

In the photo below, which was probably taken in the 1920s, Elizabeth is sitting outdoors with Bessie, the youngest of her four daughters. Elizabeth and William Robson also had four sons, the eldest of whom was Heather's father, Victor. Elizabeth was the daughter of James Elliott, born in 1814, who was a shipwright. His father, John Elliott, born in 1796, was a keelman on the River Wear.

The most obvious difference between the rug and the photo upon which it is based is Heather's introduction of color into a monochrome image, a change that was necessary to give the scene a sense of life. Heather wanted this rug to capture the quality of peace and freshness that accompanies the first light of day; the palette she has chosen creates the feeling of a misty early morning. "I used colors I like very much," she said, "in shades which allow the work to become atmospheric." Near the top of the rug, the subtle colors of the landscape fade into the near white of the sky. This echoes the way in which the grey shades of the hazy buildings on the horizon of the photo fade into the white sky surrounding them. In the sky Heather conveys a strong impression of early morning calm simply by using almost dead-straight rows of loops.

In contrast, the buildings on the horizon are not made with straight rows. Called directional hooking, this is a variation on the basic hooking technique that most rug-makers use extensively. It is partly this directional hooking that makes the buildings stand out from the sky. Despite being made of the same fabric, the more distant building on the left fades into the background because it is mostly made of the same straight rows of hooking as the sky.

The Ha'penny Ferry, fine-cut wool on even-weave Scottish hessian, 2004. 25 x 19 inches (63 x 48cm). *Collection of the artist.*

Distant buildings on the horizon.

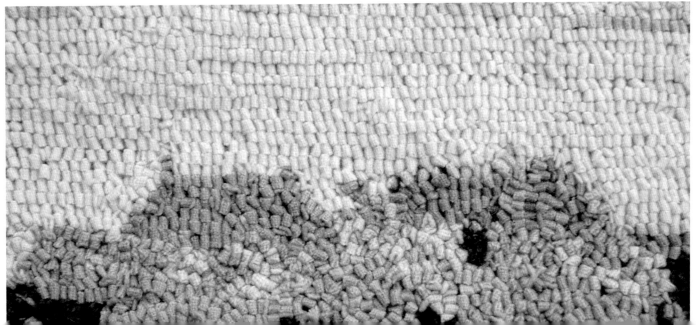

The Reverse-watercolor Principle

As a talented watercolor artist, Heather is well-placed to observe that, in some respects, the process of hooking a pictorial rug is the opposite of painting a watercolor picture. When you paint a picture, you put the wash on first and put the colors on top of the wash, she said. "You work a rug the opposite way and whatever is most important you put in first." In this rug, Heather hooked the buildings first and did not start to hook the trees and rocks that make up the background until the buildings were complete. Likewise, she finished hooking Mr. Glasper before creating his boat around him. Only then did she create the water, which supports the boat.

This method of working gives you physical space on the backing to make sure that the shapes and forms of the most important design elements are exactly right and ensures that their integrity cannot be compromised as the work progresses.

Throughout this book, Heather's naturalistic style emphasizes the importance of following the lines of the subject, the body that lies underneath clothing for example, to achieve a realistic and three-dimensional effect. Heather's approach to pictorial rug making is, in this respect as in so many others, completely unlike knitting where the design elements form part of each row and their shapes grow as you knit. (In contrast, when she is working on an Oriental rug she deliberately hooks in straight rows, working on the weft, to emulate weaving.)

Heather points out that this is just the way she approaches her pictorial work and that many people do work in straight lines to achieve particular effects. Some American artists, like Anne-Marie Littenberg for instance, paint a picture on a canvas made of fabric strips then work in a very organized way, perhaps from top left to bottom right, to recreate the original picture in quite fantastic-looking hooky. In addition, there is a whole school of rug making, the unique and beautiful Grenfell Newfoundland rugs, that are always hooked in straight lines.

The reverse-watercolor technique (*Bolton Castle*, detail of the work in progress).

The whole of *The Ha'penny Ferry* is made using hooky and, unusually for a piece of Heather's work, has a border around the picture. She explained that:

Many rug-makers, particularly from the traditional American schools, use borders which contain a lot of details around their work, but my eyes get dizzy looking at them. I am not a big fan of borders because I feel they can detract from a pictorial rug. As most of my rugs are pictorial, I usually work the picture right to the edge of the backing (excluding the margin I have allowed for finishing off the rug). There is no logical reason why I choose to add a border or not — I seem to work on instinct.

Heather's instinct was right here: the formal border of solid color she put around this rug enhances the feeling of peace that pervades it, enclosing the subject matter with tranquillity. For an example of one of Heather's rugs that has a border full of detail, see Chapter 8, *Scarcote*.

Coxgreen, where the Elliott family lived (shown here in an Edwardian postcard), is a tiny hamlet today but it has always been an important river-crossing place. The first permanent footbridge crossing of the Wear at this point was built in 1958, but when the Elliotts lived here there was only the ferry. This closed in 1956, a year before the ferry crossing at Hylton also closed.

The rowboat ferry at Coxgreen, County Durham. *Reproduced by permission of Durham County Record Office D/CI 27/278/402*

The Hylton Chain Ferry, pre-1915. *Courtesy of South Hylton Local History Society*

The Hylton Ferry, about 1930. *Courtesy of South Hylton Local History Society*

Before the A19 bridge was built, the ferry was a lifeline to the people of both parts of Hylton and the surrounding villages. The only way to cross the river with a horse and cart at this point was the chain ferry or, for foot passengers, the rowboat ferry (known locally as the "coble"), which carried on working every day until 1957.

A postcard of the chain ferry, which was published in the early 1900s, shows the buildings on the south bank of the Wear at Hylton. Now that the high A19 road bridge is the only crossing of the Wear at this point, Hylton forms two distinct communities on the north and south banks of the river.

The previous river crossing is still remembered in the name of the road, Ferryboat Lane, which runs in front of the houses shown in a view of North Hylton that probably dates from around 1930.

Heather's father, Victor, was born at Southwick, further downstream and nearer the center of Sunderland. He grew up close to the Wear, and Hylton was one of the places he played as a child.

Below the straight lines of the sky and the delicate shading of the buildings on the horizon there is a sudden change of mood. Heather introduces a

Rocks and trees on the skyline.

range of greens for the trees growing on the valley side and browns for the exposed rocks. She continues to use directional hooking to define the rocks and trees that frame the buildings lining the water's edge.

The shades of color Heather used for the buildings reflect the tones of the original photograph. She found a mixture of tweedy wools in red brick colors for the building on the left, the white building in the center is made of a variety of light-colored fabrics and the one on the right contains a mixture of stone colors. Heather drew on her training as a watercolor artist when she enhanced these basic shades with touches of blue and green.

The roofs are the cool blue-grey of slate or the deep red of clay tiles and the buildings appear to tangle around one another, almost like living things. Heather points out that the photo shows buildings which were broken down and shabby, as was much of the housing on the outskirts of Sunderland between the wars, and infers that Hylton was a poor area when it was taken.

The three riverside buildings.

A19 bridge and Golden Lion pub, South Hylton, August 2008.

Visiting the site today, it is clear that all of the buildings in the *Sunderland Echo* photo have now gone. The Golden Lion pub, which was just out of shot to the left and looked very different then, has a riverside car park and garden where the houses and the ferry waiting room (the small building just to the left of the white house in the center of the rug) once stood. The ferry steps are still visible and the A19 bridge is all too obvious, to one's eyes and ears.

When she was ready to start work on the rug, Heather first hooked straight horizontal, vertical and diagonal lines to define the shapes of the buildings, making sure that they were in proportion with one another. When she was happy with the relative positions and sizes of the buildings, she added windows and doors before she filled in the gaps between these elements to create the walls and roofs, using straight or directional hooking as best suited the subject.

Heather worked this rug on her normal reverse-watercolor principle, hooking the nearest and most prominent buildings first before starting work on those that appear to be further away. When the buildings were complete, Heather hooked the sky above them and the wooded area behind them. She then defined the shape and position of the jetty wall and completed the ground between it and the houses before turning to the ferry man, Mr. Glasper. Starting work on this figure reminded Heather of the rug's connection to her ancestors.

Like all keelmen, John Elliott's profession was named after the boat that gave him his trade. A keel was a large flat-bottomed boat powered by a punt-like pole or, less commonly, by long oars or sails, with a crew of just one or two men. Each keel could carry a large amount of coal, a quantity known as a keel of coal. John Elliott would have navigated his keel from coal-loading areas upstream on the Wear to ships waiting in the harbor downriver. These loading areas are known as staithes in this region of England, from the Norse word for landing stage. Some staithes had loading chutes to make the task of transferring the coal easier and, later, they were designed to load coal direct into ships that did away with the need for keelmen.

Keelmen were unique to the north east of England, plying their trade on both the Tyne and the Wear rivers from medieval times until the 19th century. The Wear is a comparatively shallow river that is not navigable by heavily-laden, deep-hulled ships for much of its length. Even after it was dredged in 1749, keelmen continued to play a vital role in the export of coal that was so crucial to the region's economy. The working life of a keelman was very hard.

Mr. Glasper and the other ferry men worked very hard too. In living memory it cost just half of one old penny (equivalent to about 4p or 10 US cents today) for an adult to cross the Wear in his boat, and probably half that amount for a child, so it would have taken many crossings to earn a day's wage. It must have been very heavy work when the boat held its maximum load of four or six passengers (the boats varied over time), and a dishearteningly poorly-paid task when the boat was not full. Because the ferry crossed the Wear at its narrowest point for several miles, the ebb and flow of the tidal water often produced strong currents. In the spring a great deal of extra water, known as the "fresh", runs into the river from the high ground near its source. This often carries tree trunks and other debris and the ferry would sometimes have to be taken out of the water because the crossing could be very dangerous.

Heather hooked Mr. Glasper before creating the little vessel around him. An integral part of working by the reverse-watercolor principle, this ensured that the scale of the boat did not overwhelm the hard-working man seated inside it.

Staithes and keels on the River Tyne, 1773 (detail). *Science Museum London/SSPL 10247698*

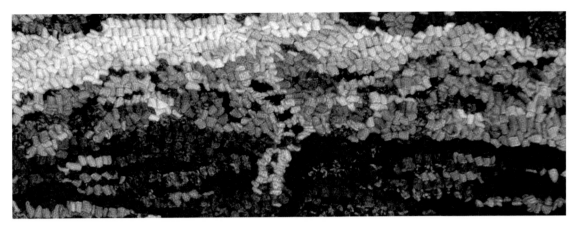

Ladder and harbor wall.

Naturally the water reflects its surroundings. Exactly as in the photo, the ladder that hangs down from the wharf into the water is reflected at an oblique angle on the water's surface.

The photograph was taken from Ferryboat Lane, North Hylton, looking towards the more populous South Hylton. Because the Wear flows from west to east, the sun would have risen over the photographer's left shoulder, bathing the buildings across the water in hazy early morning sunshine. In the turbulent watery reflections, the shapes of the buildings are lost, but their colors form swirling patterns on the surface of the water as Mr. Glasper rows his boat across the Wear.

Mr. Glasper in his boat.

Mr. Glasper, dressed in black with a white shirt, has an oar in each hand as he rows away from the viewer. The separate planks of his wooden boat are clearly visible — any less detail would be unthinkable to a rug-maker like Heather whose ancestors made their living from the shipping on this river and whose husband was in the Merchant Navy. Heather's swirling patterns of darker color reflecting the buildings replace the photograph's rather stark reflection of the boat in the water. The boat in the rug gives the impression that it is sitting comfortably on the water, that it is a sturdy little craft. You can almost see and hear drops of water spilling from the just-raised, rich-brown, wet oar blade.

Oar blade.

The ripples in the water really bring this rug alive. They do not detract from the sense of a calm and peaceful morning, but they bring movement and activity to an otherwise very still scene. Heather has used directional hooking to convey the way the water has been disturbed by the oars and the hull of the boat as it crosses the river. The contrast between the stillness of the sky with its straight lines and the movement of the water is dynamic. Each eddy and ripple on the river's surface reflects the colors of what is around it — the boat, the buildings on the river bank, the trees high up on the hillside — creating a microcosm of the rest of the rug.

Disturbed water.

The boat's crossing has brought disturbance to the water, but we can look beyond that into the future of this scene. We know that the entire width of the river will soon settle back to the apparently peaceful flatness of the water just beyond the rocks in the foreground. When that happens, those tranquil shades of white will extend across most of the width of the river again and the buildings' reflections will be disturbed only by the water's flow, until Mr. Glasper sets off in the ferry boat once more.

In the almost undisturbed water nearest the viewer, Heather uses directional hooking to simulate the endless movement of the water as it flows towards the North Sea as well as the turbulence beneath its surface when the tide turns and two conflicting bodies of water meet at this narrow crossing point. The sinuous lines are not immediately obvious because the colors are so similar one to another. Heather dyed the very pale shades she used in this rug especially for it and here they reinstate the peace of the scene after the hubbub of the disturbed water, reflecting as they do the colors of the sky.

Heather has worked this rug in pure wool, her favorite fabric for rug-making. The strips are cut very fine (see *The Reeth Parliament,* Chapter 12) and they include some tweedy fabrics, especially in the buildings and the wall of the river bank. All the strips are the same width, which enhances the tranquillity of the finished rug. Overall, *The Ha'penny Ferry* is a quiet piece and the even texture of the work adds to its peaceful nature. Because of her many links with the subject matter, it is one of Heather's favorite rugs.

Foreground rocks and ripples.

4

Victory Garden

Eleanor May and Jessie
Helen Milburn, around 1925.
Archives of the artist.

Jessie and William
Milburn, around 1925.
Archives of the artist.

William Milburn
outside the shed on his
allotment garden.

Heather created this rug to take to the USA as a demonstration piece for a class she was teaching. She wanted a rug with a north of England theme which also showed perspective. "I found a photo of my grandfather on his allotment, and that's where the idea started."

Heather's maternal grandfather, William Milburn, was born in Gateshead in 1878 and married Helen Blake, three years his junior and also a Gateshead native. Their two daughters were both born in the town; Heather's mother, Eleanor May, in 1903 and her aunt, Jessie Helen, in 1905.

The photo that inspired *Victory Garden* shows Jessie standing in front of her beloved father. William is leaning on a spade outside the shed and greenhouse on the allotment he took over when the family settled in Fulwell, on the northern edge of Sunderland. Now a city, Sunderland was a town until 1992 when it was granted city status to mark the 40th anniversary of Queen Elizabeth II's accession to the throne. Fulwell has been a formal part of Sunderland since the nineteenth century but it still feels like a village, partly thanks to its famous windmill. William is not looking at the camera. He is wearing a tie, his jacket is buttoned and he is wearing boots, as though he is impatient to start work in the garden as soon as the photograph has been taken.

The allotment system supplied most of the fresh vegetables eaten by poor people in Britain during the 19th and early 20th centuries. There are two clues that suggest that William grew vegetables for his family for reasons of pleasure, convenience and quality rather than because they were poor. The first clue is that the Milburns (or someone they knew) owned a camera and could capture a casual image at a time when many people still had to visit the formal setting of a photographer's studio if they wanted a likeness. The second clue comes from the quality of William and Jessie's clothes, which appear to be well-made, clean and tidy. Judging by the style of Jessie's dress and shoes, the photo was probably taken in the mid- to late-1920s. If that is the case, Jessie would have

Victory Garden, mixed textiles, mostly wool, on hessian, 2005. 38 x 30 inches (96 x 76cm). *Collection of the artist.*

been in her late teens or early twenties although, by the standards of the early 21st century, she looks much younger.

As Heather created *Victory Garden* she was thinking about WWII and the British government's Dig for Victory campaign that had a counterpart in the USA known as Victory Gardens. Both campaigns had the aim of reducing the amount of food that was imported. In 1918 there were around 1,500,000 allotment plots in the UK, but numbers fell during the 1920s and '30s. After the WWII campaign, the number of allotments in the UK was almost back to 1918 levels. Heather explained that "everybody needed to grow vegetables during the war and that's why they had their allotments and gardens." Dig for Victory in Britain even had a campaign song, which went: *Dig! Dig! Dig! And your muscles will grow big / Keep on pushing the spade / Don't mind the worms / Just ignore their squirms / And when your back aches, laugh with glee / And keep on diggin' / Till we give our foes a Wiggin' / Dig! Dig! Dig! to Victory.*

Dig for Victory poster. *The Imperial War Museum/PST 696*

Small flower pots on top of canes.

I wanted this rug to be different to my usual work, a bit more modern. That's why I included the big cabbages, but I also wanted to include the traditional image of pigeons coming back to their cree to roost. At the top of the rug I used colors which fade into the distance to create a feeling of perspective. The paths suggest you can walk a long way into the garden. I put in lots of my favorite things, like little plant pots on top of the canes and a wooden water butt. I included bits of glitzy fabric and used little gems and beads for the pigeons' eyes. I love pigeons — their gentle cooing voices are wonderful.

Heather loves allotments and gardens almost as much as she loves pigeons. William's allotment shed is very prominent in *Victory Garden*. Beneath its reflective windows, tomatoes made of tiny round red beads nestle snugly into their lush hooky greenery.

Tomatoes.

In the plot behind William's shed, the orange tops of carrots stick out of the soil and, two rows behind them, the fleshy subtle green leaves of leeks stand high above the rich brown earth. Both of these impressions are created using cut high loops. Heather has left the high loops uncut in the clumps of lettuce behind the leeks.

You may not see these vegetables as lettuces or leeks and Heather would not mind at all. She has simply created a general impression of a range of types of vegetable rather than laboring over the details to produce specific and accurate representations. Of course, sometimes an accurate portrayal is useful or important in a rug. One of the beauties of rug-making is that it gives you the flexibility to produce precise images or general impressions to suit different interpretations of an endless range of subjects.

Heather may not have depicted specific vegetables, but the wide variety she has suggested gives an impression of William Milburn's great productivity and industry. The rug suggests that he spent Sunday afternoons and warm summer evenings digging, weeding, watering and harvesting on this plot before carrying the produce home in a wheelbarrow or a basket to Helen, Eleanor May and Jessie.

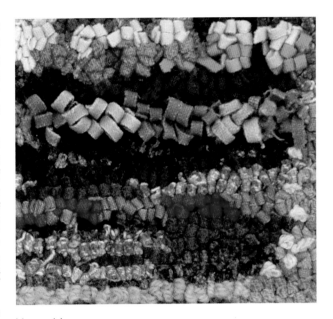

Vegetables.

Vegetables.

Rose hips and apples from Heather's garden on the bench outside Greencroft's back door.

The largest and most detailed vegetables Heather has planted in William's allotment are, as she pointed out, the cabbages. These are important elements in helping to create the impression of perspective. Heather made them from high loops, both cut and uncut, in a variety of widths. She cut the fine loops of light-colored fabric in their centers to produce a dome-shaped mound. This could be seen as the densely-packed heart of a cabbage or even as the frothy, foam-like center of a cauliflower. She left the larger, darker loops around the center uncut to simulate loose outer leaves.

Heather has used a very wide range of greens in this rug, a far greater variety than you could buy in the best-stocked fabric or charity shops. Because green is always the most difficult color to find in new

Cabbages.

or recycled fabric, Heather often dyes white fabric or over-dyes colored fabrics to produce the shades of green she needs. Apart from the glitzy highlights, virtually all the fabrics in *Victory Garden* are wool, and Heather dyed many of them using her favorite acid dyes. The range of greens in the cabbages gives a good idea of the hard work that goes into dyeing the fabrics for one of Heather's pictorial rugs; luckily, she loves to work with wool, whatever the task.

Heather also dyed fabrics for the soil and the paths. In the area just to the right of the cabbages, for instance, an astonishing variety of brown came from one piece of flannel. She created this unique piece, and the many others used in the rugs in this book, by dip and casserole dyeing in random spots, techniques that produce a rich spectrum of tailor-made colors unobtainable any other way. These techniques are invaluable and they will be explained later.

The path.

Flannel

"Flannel" is the word Heather uses to describe the plain-weave woollen cloth she prefers to use for pictorial rugs. Flannel is essentially a soft fabric woven from loosely-spun carded wool and it does not have a nap (pile direction). Modern flannel often has a partly synthetic make-up and Heather is careful to buy only pure wool flannel. (Flannelette is an entirely different fabric that Heather would not normally use because it is brushed cotton.)

Pure wool flannel readily takes up the acid dyes Heather prefers and is a marvellous vehicle for the casserole, spot and dip dyeing techniques which she uses to such good effect.

For more information about cutting fabrics and the various weaves suitable for rug-making, see Chapter 5, *The Evacuees*. For more information about dyeing, see Chapter 6, *Percival's Bus* (dip dyeing) and Chapter 11, *Reeth Village Green* (spot and casserole dyeing).

Samples of pure wool flannel acid-dyed by Heather.

When the piece of flannel was dry, Heather cut the fabric into strips on the grain, as is essential for most woollen cloths. (Some tweeds must be cut on the cross and some can be cut straight. As with so many aspects of rug-making, Heather suggests that you experiment with the fabric you want to use to see which cutting method works best.) The resulting series of strips of fabric contained a wide range of shades; every time Heather pulled a loop through the backing she introduced a slightly different color into the mix.

Heather used glitzy fabrics to good effect in this rug, with tiny sparkling loops highlighting the pigeons' breasts as well as some of the vegetables. It is not hard to imagine that a recent shower from William's watering can (filled from the butt alongside his shed) has left drops of glittering water in the curling leaves of the runner beans on their poles.

Wooden water butt.

William's wonderful cabbages are a very important design element, and the large pigeons are equally prominent. To create the rug, Heather started with a blank sheet of paper. She positioned the basic items she wanted to include and produced lots of preliminary sketches. "I wanted to create a garden in a rug, so where did I start? Anywhere! My only rule is that the design must be pleasing to the eye, and that means it must be balanced. I don't normally want any single feature to shout out at me," she said.

The pigeons are balanced, both in colors and as design elements, by their cree. Heather's cree is based on one in a painting by Jimmy Floyd, a member of the Ashington Group of artists. This painting is called *Pigeon Crees* and its influence on Heather's work is obvious. Heather has reversed the direction of the cree to suit the rug.

Jimmy Floyd's cree is typical of those found in the north of England. The short wooden picket fence along the top of the front wall of the cree has become, in Heather's interpretation, almost like crenellations on a castle.

The fluffy threads below the cree are one of Heather's trademarks, lengths of un-spun Swaledale fleece which she added when the rug was nearly finished. "They're just a bit of fun," she said, explaining "in a sense, I draw with fabric and this is an artwork made from recycled blankets and sweaters. I try to make every rug different and, even though I always try to come up with new ideas, I nearly always use a bit of fleece, plain or dyed, somewhere in every rug."

Most of the small pigeons are embellished with embroidery thread that Heather added as a finishing touch after the hooking work was more or less completed. At that point in the process, she made French-knot vegetables and, for the birds' eyes, she sewed on tiny dark beads that catch the light and sparkle. These are just some of the many techniques she uses to enhance the already-richly-detailed picture that a simple hooky rug creates. "On the back of this rug you can see where I have added the embroidery elements, and the line of the path is really clear," said Heather.

Runner beans.

Pigeon cree.

French knots.

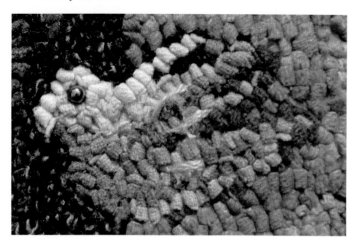

Small pigeon.

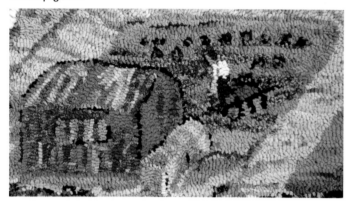

Distant plot with cold frames and wheelbarrow.

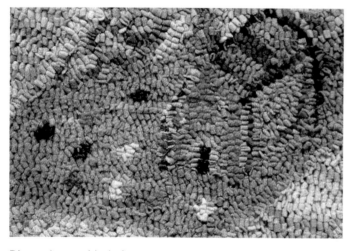

Distant hens with their coop.

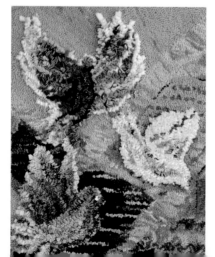

Three large pigeons.

Apart from William, whose outline she traced, most of *Victory Garden* came from Heather's imagination. Having established the all-important vanishing point, she worked freehand as she drew the lines of the paths and the plots. She then placed, between these directional lines, the outlines of the sheds and the cree, and the positions of the cabbages and the large pigeons. Because this is a hooky rug, Heather drew the design on the front of the hessian.

The large pigeons bring a strong impression of movement to the rug and it is easy to see how high above the allotment they are. Heather has achieved her goal of creating a piece with a strong perspective in *Victory Garden*. Her use of receding shades of the same palette of colors heightens the sense of perspective which she created with clear lines leading to a definite vanishing point and enhanced by the decreasing size of the design elements, like the man and his wheelbarrow in one of the farthest plots. As with the small vegetables in William's plot, the figure is suggested rather than being highly detailed. The body language is enough to tell you that this is a hardworking man and your imagination does the rest.

Heather uses the word "jizz" when describing this: according to the *Concise Oxford Dictionary*, jizz is "the characteristic impression given by an animal or plant," although that definition can surely be extended to include any inanimate object that has a distinct shape or design. In this area of *Victory Garden*, Heather's understanding of jizz shows in the gardener, his wheelbarrow and some nearby hens.

Hens are another of the loves of Heather's life and are creatures she knows well. Feathers and combs, feet and wings are all there in the jizz in the most distant plot in this rug; this looks exactly like a hen house whose occupants are all busy scratching at the soil, despite the colors being among the palest Heather has used. Compare their hen coop and the neat shed on the next plot, which has cold frames along one side, with William's shed; each section of the allotment garden looks quite different to the others, reflecting the different purposes to which their owners put their plots.

The large pigeons, which are finely detailed and have directional hooking to define their body parts and feathers, are formed of hooky loops like the rest of this piece of work. Some of them are cut high, which can produce a shaggy, feathery effect, very appropriate for these pigeons. The loops can be cut as you work to ensure that you are achieving the effect you want.

Cut high loops

Cut high loops are made exactly as their name suggests: pull loops of fabric higher than those in the surrounding work and cut through them to produce two flying ends per loop. These ends can be the same length or one can be left longer than the other, depending on the effect you want to achieve. You can shear all of their tops off at once, as Heather has done in the cabbages and pigeons, which leads to even heights and a very neat appearance. Alternatively, you can cut through the tops of the loops one at a time, perhaps angling your cut slightly to achieve different heights and/or angles on the ends.

In the first photo below, Heather is making cut loops using a smaller hook than would normally be the case for fabric of that width. This mismatch leads to the fabric becoming folded over the hook and, when you shear the top off, you reveal a little curl in the loop. The third photo shows the difference between working with a hook appropriate to the size of the loop (top) and an undersized one (bottom).

You can also leave the high loops intact and you will spot many examples of the ways Heather uses high loops, cut in various ways or left uncut, in this book.

Make all the high loops in one part of your design before you cut them. If you need to re-work the area after you cut them, you are in for a lot more work than just tugging on the end of a strip which can then be re-used.

If you use wider strips to create cut high loops they will naturally flop about and fold over, which can look perfect for plants or hair, for instance. If you use a wide strip to make closely-spaced high loops that you then cut quite short, you will get tight little curls that show clearly where the strips were folded over. This is used to good effect in *Jackdaw Jeans* (see *My Animals and Other Family Members,* Chapter 14) and it has many other creative applications.

In this technique the only limit to your creativity is your imagination; mastering the basic hooky technique will unleash it. You have nothing to lose but a little strip of fabric, so it is always worth experimenting. As Heather has found to her delight, you can have a lot of fun carrying out experiments with fabrics as your expertise in hooking progresses. You will not know how a fabric will work until you use it. It is great fun to find out through trial and error, processes Heather loves to explore in rug-making.

Heather points out that, despite their similarity to proddy, cut loops made with fine fabrics are not suitable for use in floor rugs because the strips are much shorter than proddy strips and they are not as stable. Using thick fabrics will make short cut loops more secure, and therefore suitable for floor rugs, because they will fit more tightly into the backing. You could make an entire rug using cut high loops, shearing them off when the work is complete, but you must use thick fabrics to keep the cut loops secure. If you used an undersized hook, your work would then be full of little curls that would give it a lovely texture.

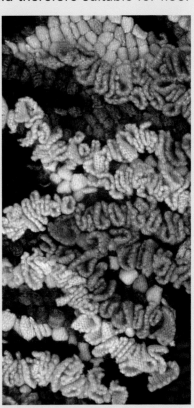

Cut high loops: detail of *Jackdaw Jeans.*

Cut high loops: forming curled over loops, shearing the tops, finished.

Why has Heather used cut high loops instead of proddy, another common technique used for rug-making that uses a short strip and leaves two flying ends on the front of the rug? (The proddy technique is explained in Chapter 16, *Paradise Garden*.) Heather says that she loves the speed of working with hooky and the even result she gets. She also enjoys the way her hand-dyed fabrics produce subtle gradations of color in hooky, an effect it would take a great deal of effort to achieve in proddy. By cutting through hooky loops she simulates the appearance of almost impossibly tight and very well-organized proddy work while keeping all the advantages of hooky.

Naturally, Heather does make good use of proddy when it is appropriate to the work, such as the shaped form used in *Origins and Identity*, Chapter 18. Cut high loops produce a result that cannot be obtained through proddy work. Proddy strips need to be much wider than fine hooky strips to avoid fraying, and they are normally much more widely spaced on the background.

The colors Heather chose for the pigeons, mostly soft greys and creams with touches of muted browns as well as some violets and deep blue (including a bit of glitzy fabric), are typical of the type of fantail pigeons her son Laurence kept at one time. Although

Looking across the leeks and carrots.

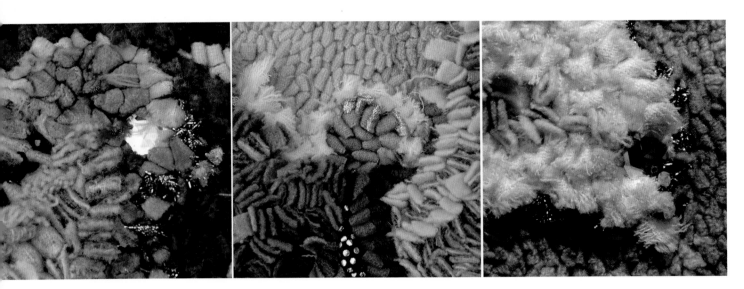

The heads of the three large pigeons.

Looking across the pigeons.

some of these colors are similar to the pastel shades of the receding background, they stand out from it because of the texture of the work.

The pigeons offer a valuable insight into Heather's reverse-watercolor method of working. She hooked them onto blank hessian and only put the allotment plots in behind them when she was completely happy with the birds' appearance.

Trying to work the other way round, by leaving a space to fill in later with something important, is asking for trouble. You simply cannot be sure how the element you want to put into the space will look until you start to work on it. You might need to undo some of the background if the hole is too small, or the shape might end up squashed and wrong. I work this way because it is so much easier in the long run to get the most important bits of the mat right to start with.

One of the great joys of rug-making, Heather tells her students, is that when something does not look right you can remove loops and re-hook it until you are completely happy. This actually happened during the writing of this book. When Heather saw the close-up photo of William outside his shed in an early draft, she realized that she was not happy with his figure and spent some time changing it. The new William in these photos was created four years after the rest of the rug.

Victory Garden will last a long time because, like almost all of her work, Heather used wools to create it. For a commissioned piece she would normally use a linen backing but, in every other respect, she takes the same amount of care over all the work she creates.

Laurence had some fantail pigeons when we moved to Hurst, high up on the moors above Reeth, and they moved with us. Laurence was a real bird lover, a member of the junior RSPB, and we ended up with a barn full of pigeons because the vets and other people used to bring him injured birds. His fantails bred with the wild pigeons and we ended up with a right motley crew; somebody may have culled them by now.

That sad thought is balanced by knowing that Heather has depicted so many of the things she loves in this rug and that the pigeons will forever fly free in the sky above William's allotment, his Victory Garden.

Large pigeon.

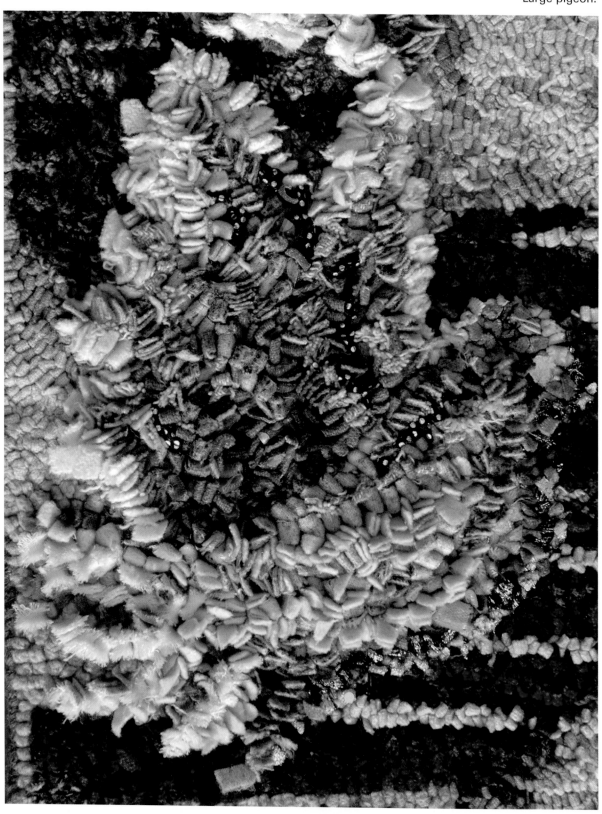

wearing black plimsolls or dusty boots. The boy in the front row with the small suitcase is carrying his gas mask slung on a string across his chest. It is unlikely that he would have needed it in his new home, but the journey started in Sunderland, which was under threat of gas attack, and carrying them was obligatory. His gas mask is in a very special shiny tin; they were issued in far-from-sturdy cardboard boxes.

Government guidance on privately arranged evacuations, such as that enjoyed by the Robson family, (said in Public Information Leaflet No. 3 issued from the Lord Privy Seal's Office in July 1939):

If you have made private arrangements for getting away your children [sic] to relatives or friends in the country, or intend to make them, you should remember that while the Government evacuation scheme is in progress ordinary railway and road services will necessarily be drastically reduced and subject to alteration at short notice. Do not, therefore, in an emergency leave your private plans to be carried out at the last moment. It may then be too late.

The threat to children was very real and the fear in those cities at greatest risk of bombing would have been overwhelming.

Drawing straight onto the backing

When creating a rug, whatever the subject matter and whether it has come from her imagination or uses another image as its source, Heather always starts by drawing a series of sketches of the design. When she is happy that she has found a location for everything she wants to include in the rug, it is time to transfer the design to the backing. She has two ways to do this:

1. If the item which forms the focus of the design can be photocopied, Heather will use the "trace and transfer" method, which is explained in Chapter 12, *The Reeth Parliament*.

2. If the item cannot be photocopied, she uses a grid to create the enlargement. She also uses a lightbox if she has a difficult or complicated pattern to copy, such as an Oriental rug. Les built a lightbox for her, a wooden frame that surrounds a short neon tube and supports a piece of toughened glass. It is an endlessly useful device.

If Heather is working entirely from her imagination, there is obviously no source material she needs to copy. After creating the design on paper, Heather lays a transparent grid over it. She then uses a stick of chalk to draw a grid on a piece of hessian of the right size for the rug, including the borders for finishing. The last step is to copy the design, freehand and full-size, onto the backing. When the chalk drawing replicates her paper drawing to her satisfaction, she goes over the design lines with a black, felt-tip pen to commit the basic elements of the design to the backing; chalk alone would brush away as you work.

Regardless of the method used, you always draw the design on the front of your backing for hooky work and on the back for proddy work. (There is more about proddy in Chapter 16, *Paradise Garden*.) Remember that the lines you draw are only a guide; you can hook or prod over them to alter the design as you work on it.

Heather's lightbox: she has pinned the line drawing with the backing fabric on top of it to the wood. You can see the original (left), the process (right) with the enlarged drawing illuminated from below, and the finished drawing on the backing (center, resting on a piece of obscure material for clarity).

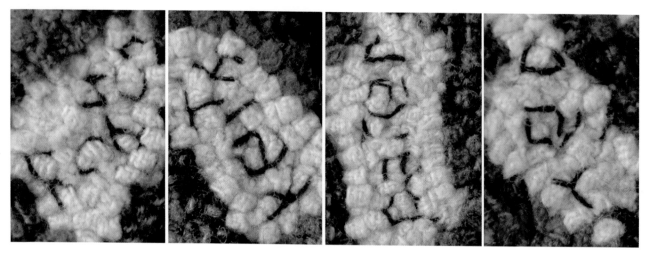

The four labels: Robson, Keith, Peter and Teddy.

Apart from having one sock higher than the other, like several of these boys, the one thing the Robson brothers have in common with all of the Sunderland evacuees is a label. Each child evacuated under Operation Pied Piper carried an ID card or had a luggage label tied with string to a suitable part of their clothing, to the few possessions they clutched so tightly or slung around their neck. The information given on these labels varied widely between the regions evacuated. While some labels were partly pre-printed, others were entirely hand-written. All of the labels were intended to carry the child's full name and home address and the name of the school from which they were being evacuated. Few families had a telephone at home at the outbreak of WWII so there probably would not have been a contact phone number. The boys on the right of Heather's source material have their labels clearly displayed, one on a loop of string around his neck and the other tied to his coat.

Heather has labelled each boy in *The Evacuees,* even though as private evacuees their mother was obliged to make their own travel and accommodation arrangements and they would not have needed those labels. In doing so, Heather is using her brothers to represent all the 3.5 million people who were evacuated in Great Britain during WWII. Over what must have been an astonishingly busy three days at the start of the war, 827,000 individually-labelled, school-age children were evacuated school-by-school, with 103,000 teachers and other helpers. At the same time, 524,000 mothers and children under five, 13,000 pregnant women and 7,000 disabled people (a total of almost 1.5 million people) were evacuated.

All too often, children who were evacuated without their parents were forced to live under terrible circumstances. In order to escape the abuse and deprivation some evacuated children suffered in the so-called "safe areas", and because some of them were dreadfully homesick, many children undertook dangerous solo journeys to return home or were removed by their parents after they sent messages home, begging for rescue. Because they returned to the danger areas before the threat of bombing had passed, there were some tragic deaths as a result.

Shorter, younger, dark-haired Keith.

Keith and Peter both appear to have their labels tied through buttonholes in their jackets. Peter's teddy bear is labelled too; it would be a disaster to arrive at your strange new home without the comfort of your favorite toy.

There is no photograph of the Robson boys leaving Sunderland, so Heather has simply adapted the photo by adding some of her brothers' characteristics. As she put it, "one of them was small and dark and the other one was fair." *The Evacuees* shows two sweet-looking boys, and Heather's much-loved brothers may have decided for themselves whether Peter and Keith are actually meant to represent them in any other way than the names on the labels.

Taller, older, light-haired Peter.

The Clark's shipyard crane stood high over the River Wear.

Heather made this rug on a hessian backing using her favorite fabric, wool, and it is worked entirely in hooky. The sky and the buildings in front of it, the wall behind the boys and the ground beneath their feet are all created using more-or-less straight rows, a regimentation which reinforces the industrial feel of the piece. Working on the reverse-watercolor principle, Heather completed the main focus of the work before starting any of the other areas. The boys and the possessions they are taking away with them are hooked directionally, unlike the area immediately around them. This fundamental difference in the way Heather has created the boys makes them stand out from the background, even though the palette of colors is very similar. By hooking the main subjects first and then putting in the background around them, Heather ensured that the shapes and proportions of the boys are correct.

Heather has also used directional hooking for the symbols of those things that made Sunderland the place it then was: the Clark's shipyard crane represents Sunderland's long history of shipbuilding, the chimneys standing above factories making paper, chemicals and beer, the pit-head winding gear dominating the Wear colliery, and the Pyrex sign on Jobling's glass factory. All of these industries have virtually disappeared from Sunderland now and, in that sense, they too could be called evacuees. As well as being depicted in this rug, it is wonderful that the foundations of the city of Sunderland are remembered and celebrated in the marvellous open air museum at Beamish and in the fascinating National Glass Centre on the north bank of the Wear. This museum, opened in 1998, stands very close to the place where the first glass in Sunderland was made in the late seventh century, for windows of the Wearmouth-Jarrow Priory.

Heather made this rug using what she calls "shipyard industrial" colors. There are touches of brightness, notably in the boys' clothing, but most of the colors are muted brown and dark red, beige, grey and pale blue. All of the strips in the background elements are the same width, and Heather has reserved her use of narrower strips for the highly-detailed central section.

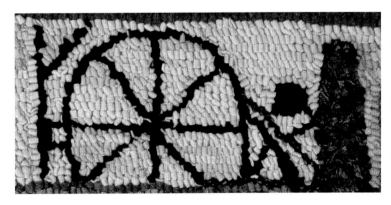

The old winding gear stood alongside the more modern winding tower above the Wearmouth colliery in the center of Sunderland.

Strip cutting

Heather uses two main methods to cut strips of fabric for rug-making. The most basic method of strip cutting uses scissors, but it is hard to keep the edges parallel and it is a very slow method. Heather says, from personal experience, "it produces terrible wear and tear on the hands." Heather's simplest method uses a hand-held rotary cutting wheel, a cutting board, and a transparent grid or ruler.

Establish the grain direction

Before you start cutting, you need to establish the grain direction of the fabric. It is easy to check this by doing a "nip and rip": this is a tiny cut through one edge followed by a tearing pull across the fabric. A strip cut along the grain is essential for most fabrics (there is more information later in this chapter on page 42 about weaves and grain) and it is not normally important whether your fabric strips have straight weft or warp grain.

Recycled fabric (where you do not usually have a selvedge to guide you) is likely to tear more easily along the lengthwise warp, because the interwoven weft threads are prone to "give" more easily under the pressure you exert as you pull. The warp threads are more stable and less inclined to stretch than the weft threads, simply because they are held under tension while the fabric is being woven. With new fabrics, you will most often cut through a selvedge, which means your straight grain is a weft direction. Whichever grain direction you end up with, it is important to get a straight edge before you start cutting straight-grain strips.

Make sure you have a straight edge

Line your newly-established straight edge up with one of the lines marked on your cutting board and align the edge of your transparent cutting grid with the first ¼ inch (6mm) mark from the straight edge. It is really important to press down firmly on the transparent grid on top of the fabric with your non-cutting hand to prevent the fabric and/or the grid moving.

Cutting the length of strip Heather likes to use — up to 14 inches (35.5cm) long — demands a steady hand and a careful eye. You need to be able to keep the fabric and the grid completely still to ensure that the strip you cut has parallel edges. This method is quick and easy for fairly wide strips, whether they are straight grain or bias, and for cutting thicker fabrics. You can also use this method to cut long strips that you later cut into short lengths for proddy work.

Bias-cut strips

Bias-cut strips will always stretch, and some bias-cut fabrics will curl in on themselves if you pull on their ends after you cut the fabric into strips. You can create special effects by exploiting this tendency. As with almost every aspect of rug-making, you can learn a lot by experimenting. If you find a new type of fabric, play with it to find out more about what you could do with it. Heather says you should never be afraid to play with your fabrics, to get to know them and their properties: you may be pleasantly surprised.

To cut bias strips, set your transparent grid at 45° to the straight edge before making your first cut. Depending on the shape of your piece of fabric, each strip is likely to be a different length to the previous one. Continue to make parallel cuts until the strips are too short to be useful.

Some fabrics must be cut on the bias, especially some of the kilts and tweedy fabrics that Heather is so fond of using. See *A word about weaves* (page 42) in this chapter for an explanation of why this is important.

Fine strips

For fine strips, Heather most often uses a hand-cranked rotary cutter. This is a quick, simple and very accurate method, but initially much more costly. The cutter has a series of interchangeable discs to produce strips of different widths. After clamping the machine to a firm horizontal surface, feed in the fabric and make sure you keep its edge parallel to the cutting wheel while turning the handle. Out will come even strips.

Top to bottom: cutting a hooky strip with scissors; cutting a strip into proddy pieces; using a block to cut several proddy strips at the same time; using a cutting wheel, board and transparent guide (along the grain); cross-cut strips; knitted fabrics stretch without shredding; the strip on the left is as cut, the strip on the right has been stretched and it curled over on itself; using a cutting machine to produce three fine strips at once.

The boys are only loosely based on the *Sunderland Echo* photo, so Heather did not need to enlarge and trace them. The buildings are invented generic riverside industrial buildings, although this *Sunderland Echo* photograph of Union Street market just before it closed in 1956 features some buildings that look very similar to Heather's invented ones. That is hardly surprising; she grew up in Sunderland and lived the early part of her life alongside scenes like this.

Union Street market, Sunderland, September 1956. *Courtesy of Sunderland Echo*

Keith's grey school blazer.

The equally fictitious boys are beautifully detailed and finely crafted. Each boy is wearing a jacket made of tweedy wools: Keith's is a grey school blazer and Peter's is a longer, heavier coat. This confirms that Heather was thinking about children older than her brothers, as Peter and Keith had not yet started school when they left Sunderland. But this, to Heather, is the essence of a memory rug: it does not need to be an exact replica of something, especially something you did not witness. An impression of how it might have been is enough to stir memories.

Apart from their coats, whose collars, buttons and sleeve creases are very carefully defined, the boys are similarly dressed. Peter is wearing short grey trousers held up with what looks like a brown leather belt. Keith's shorts are black and Heather has added grey creases to show where they have become baggy at the front, as the result of constant wear. Each boy is properly fitted out for this life-changing event with a shirt and tie, knee-length socks, and what look like black leather sandals. There are differences between the boys, despite the many similarities: Peter looks a little slimmer than Keith and, reflecting the real boys, Keith has darker hair than Peter. Their socks, with a patterned band around the top, mirror almost exactly some in the photo. And, like those boys, neither Peter

Keith's socks and shoes.

Peter's green coat.

Peter's socks and shoes.

nor Keith looks worried at the prospect of evacuation, perhaps treating it as an adventure.

From Heather's telling of the story, it is clear that her brothers had an idyllic time in Swaledale and Arkengarthdale. They attended the tiny Arkengarthdale village school (which still only had 30 pupils aged four to 11 in 2007). When they were out of school, they spent their time playing in the fields and woods. The local lads treated the Robson boys as exotic foreign visitors and they were given a very warm welcome.

Ben Wicks wrote a fascinating book, *No Time to Wave Goodbye* (published by Bloomsbury in the UK), about the mass evacuation of British children during WWII. In this book, adults recalled their childhood experiences of being evacuated. One contributor, John Aitchison, had been in a similar situation to Peter and Keith, having been evacuated from an industrial northern environment (Newcastle upon Tyne) to Swaledale. John described how he and his pals "made friends immediately with the local boys, who were captivated by our accents."

Peter and Keith's Sunderland accents would probably have been completely impenetrable to the Yorkshire lads, to start with at least, just as the local accents were hard for the Robson boys to understand when they first moved to the dale. Apparently the two groups had great fun being rude to and about each other, using words and phrases that their parents did not understand.

Even simple words like "yes" were different: Peter and Keith would agree by saying "way'ay man" and their new friends simply said "aye." When the Sunderland lads said "ha'way" it meant "come on," and when the Yorkshire boys said "ay-up" to Peter and Keith they meant "hello." This potential language barrier was partly a reflection of the fact that previous generations were not as mobile as we are today. Even as recently as the early 1940s it is likely that someone from Swaledale might only go to Sunderland a few times during their life. They did not need to make the journey, which would have been difficult at a time when very few people owned cars, because there was a much greater range of goods for sale in the shops in small towns and villages.

The bear is a lovely detail in this rug. He hangs by his right paw from Peter's left hand, his other limbs as straight as a teddy's limbs ever are. Heather defined his body clearly with just a few lines of hooky before filling in his other features, using a variety of colors to distinguish them. He is very realistic and eye-catching as he stares straight out of the rug, the round swell of his tummy reminiscent of Ernest Shepherd's drawings of Winnie the Pooh. He is made entirely of yarn, which gives him great warmth and makes him look cuddly. Because the yarn fibers tend to blend

together, it forms gently rounded loops. Using yarn in a rug brings softness to represent a characteristic which is appropriate for a teddy bear.

Sections of two very old rugs of Heather's, which are not included in this book, demonstrate that difference vividly. Despite being used in straight lines of hooky, they look different: the flannel at the top produces clearly-defined rows of loops with squared edges, while the rows of yarn below are less clear and each loop is rounded.

Peter's carefully-labelled teddy bear stares out of the rug as he hangs by one arm.

These two very old rugs demonstrate the difference in texture obtained by using yarn (front) and flannel (rear).

a word about weaves – a guide to their identification and use

This tiny sample of *Paradise Garden* contains at least three different types of fabric – three different dyed green fabrics and a salmon pink fabric, all woven; two green yarns; both the front and reverse of a pink and silver knitted glitzy fabric.

Plain-weave

Plain-weave (also known as tabby weave) is the most basic of the three main types of weave and is strong and hardwearing. In plain-weave the warp and weft form a simple crisscross pattern: each weft thread goes over one warp thread then crosses under the next, and so on. The adjacent weft thread reverses the pattern, passing under the warp threads the first one went over, etc. Rug backings are nearly always made of plain-weave, as are the flannels Heather loves to use (although the type of monk's cloth used for rug making has pairs of warp and weft threads in a plain weave pattern). For rug-making, you must always cut your strips of plain-weave fabric on the straight grain to prevent the strip stretching and shredding.

Satin-weave

Satin-weave fabric always has a lustrous appearance and a feel that can be described as silky. Because it is woven using fine threads, satin weave fabric is not normally an appropriate textile from which to make an entire rug. It can be used in small quantities for highlights, and Heather regularly uses what she calls "glitzy fabrics", some of which are satin weave. In this book there are examples in the birds flying above her *Victory Garden* (Chapter 4) as well as some of the flowers in *Paradise Garden* (Chapter 16).

Twill-weave

Twill-weave, on the other hand, is perfect for making all the pile of a rug, provided you identify it correctly and treat it appropriately. Heather's favorite cloth, tweed, is a twill-weave fabric, and a lovely story explains how tweed got its name. Apparently the fabric was called "tweel", the Scots name for "twill", until about 1830. At that time a firm in Hawick, just over the Scottish border from Northumberland (England), wrote to a London merchant about some "tweels". The merchant misread the writing and assumed the word was "tweed" and that it was a trade-name. The River Tweed flows through the Scottish Borders textile areas, so that was a reasonable assumption. He advertised the goods as "tweed", and the name stuck.

You can recognise twill by its characteristic pattern of parallel diagonal ribs, known as the "wale" of the fabric. This is the result of passing the weft thread over one or more warp threads and then under two or more warp threads, and so on. There is a "step" or offset between rows that creates the wale. Twill-weave fabrics, like herringbone tweed, kilts, etc, must be cut "on the cross", following these diagonal lines, to produce bias-cut strips. This will reduce the amount of shredding and disintegration that would otherwise occur. Denim is an example of one of the very few twill-weave fabrics from which Heather has yet to make an entire rug. Some of her students have done lovely work with the material, exploiting the wide variety of shades of blue as well as the differences between the front and back of the fabric. Heather says that working in denim is very hard on the hands and, for that reason, she does not use it. The jeans in *Jackdaw Jeans* (see Chapter 14) are made of sweaters, for instance.

A corner of Heather's garden studio in Reeth with baskets of strips and fleece, and three rugs: (foreground) *Midnight Garden* and (hanging) *Paradise Garden* (foreground) and *The Ha'penny Ferry* (behind baskets).

Knitted fabric

Knitted fabric is not woven, of course, and dressmaking velvet comes into this category. Heather loves to use velvet in rugs, but points out that it must be dressmaking velvet whose backing is knitted, not furnishing velvet, which is on a woven backing. The distinctive appearance of knitted fabric means it is easy to cut both ways, parallel to the knitting stitches or diagonally across them. Cutting from side to side along the rows of knitting (or diagonally across them) produces a stretchy strip, rather like bias-cut plain-weave fabric, which can be pulled into a secure thin strip. If you do pull on it, this strip will tend to curl in on itself, hiding the cut edges, which makes it ideal for very fine work. By warm-washing knitted fabrics before cutting them (as you should wash all fabrics you use for rug-making) you will achieve a slight felting of the fibers. This will help knitted fabrics to remain intact when cut into strips, whichever way you cut them.

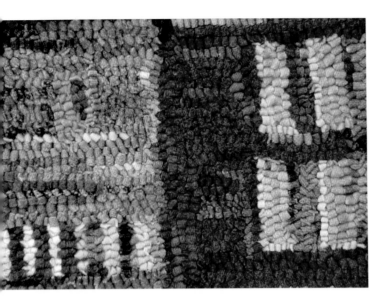

Detail of two of the buildings.

Detail of the wall behind the boys.

Heather added the lettering to the labels when the rug was finished. The names are embroidered using fine black yarn and the shapes of the letters are determined by the hooky loops between and around which they are worked.

In contrast with some other rugs (in particular *Reeth Village Green,* Chapter 11), Heather has chosen to define the buildings in *The Evacuees* as blocks of color rather than by using dark outlines. In common with every building she has put into a rug, Heather first hooked those parts of the buildings that define their shape and dimensions — the outline of the walls, roof and windows — before filling in the spaces in between — the bricks, the slates and the glass. This is the simplest way to ensure that the buildings fit together properly into the scene. You can re-work the dimensions easily if all you have committed to the backing is their outlines.

The wall behind the boys is a good demonstration of how to use color to create shapes out of straight rows of hooking. Heather has cleverly exploited a narrow range of colors to create a complex pattern. This wall appears to be made of even-sized stones piled one on top of another and held together with mortar, unlike the dry stone walls of the Yorkshire Dales. It even looks like there is soot sitting on some of the lines of mortar, presumably deposited there by smoke belching from many factory chimneys around the town.

The Evacuees is different from most of the other rugs Heather has made simply because of its subject matter. It is not "pretty", nor does it contain rural scenes of hills and dales. Heather made it partly for that very reason, as a challenge to herself to make a pictorial rug in a style completely unlike that for which she is so well-known. In comparison to the other rugs in this book, for instance, its subject matter is strikingly urban.

The story of Peter, Keith and Eleanor May's evacuation from urban Sunderland to the rural peace of Scarcote and Brookside is a vital part of the story of Heather's life in rugs. Without their evacuation and the family's subsequent return visits, Heather would not have moved to live in Reeth. Nor would she have met two wonderful women who taught her rug-making. One of them passed on a craft that she, in turn, had learned locally and the other woman brought color and fine work into Heather's rug-making. This is part of the story that is told in Chapter 11, *Reeth Village Green*.

6

Percival's Bus

Percival's Bus tells an important chapter in the story of Heather's life and is another of her memory rugs, made to capture an un-photographed moment.

By 1944, Heather's mother, Eleanor May, and her brothers Peter and Keith had lived as evacuees in Swaledale and Arkengarthdale for four years. Victor, Eleanor May's husband, had visited them many times and Eleanor May was delighted to discover that she was pregnant again. She decided to return to Sunderland to reunite her two sons with their father before the new baby's birth. In August 1944, the three of them boarded a Percival's bus in Reeth and headed back to Victor and the family's home. Sitting in the bus as it waited to drive east along Swaledale at the start of their journey, Eleanor May waved a fond farewell to her new friends. As they set off and Fremington gave way to Grinton, she gazed at the hills crowned with purple heather and stroked her bump, choosing the name she would give the baby if it were a girl. Heather was born the following November.

Heather's love of the dales is something she has carried with her all her life. She said, "Since I was a little girl I have felt a strong attraction to the dales, and I love the sea too. Now that I can get to and from Sunderland in an hour I have the best of both worlds."

Arkengarthdale, late 1940s: Heather's father Victor stands between her mother Eleanor May, on the right, and Eleanor May's great friend from Langthwaite who was known as Auntie Didi. Peter (left) and Keith (right) stand in front of their parents while the superb scenery of the Yorkshire Dales rolls away behind the group. *Archives of the artist*

LODGE PERCIVAL,
GUNNERSIDE, Richmond, Yks.
....
Grocer and Flour Dealer,
Cake Merchant,
Cheese and Bacon Factor.
....
MOTOR PROPRIETOR.
DAILY SERVICE TO RICHMOND.
DARLINGTON MONDAYS. :: :: :: ::
:: :: :: :: PRIVATE CARS FOR HIRE.

This advertisement for Lodge Percival appeared in the program for the Swaledale Agricultural Society's Annual Show at Muker in 1925.

Lodge Percival, Motor Proprietor, advertised passenger services in the 1925 programme for the Swaledale Agricultural Society's Annual Show at Muker. The bus that Eleanor and the boys caught in 1944 was part of a fully-fledged service with a daily route to Richmond and Darlington. Percival had a fleet of distinctive cream and maroon vehicles proudly bearing the company name.

The name of the proprietor appears below the round-topped window at the back of the bus.

Percival's Bus, fine-cut wool on white linen, 2001. 22 x 16 inches (55 x 40cm). *Collection of the artist*

This postcard from 1955 shows a view of Reeth which is almost unchanged today, except for the number and type of vehicles. *Copyright The Francis Frith Collection*

Heather used this 1955 postcard of a Percival's bus on the green in Reeth as her source, and uses this example to stress that you do not need to be able to draw to make a rug. Adapting an existing image, as she did here, can give you the main focus and, by adding your choice of details, real or imaginary, you can make up your own picture.

Introducing color into a monochrome image when you do not know what the original colors were obviously involves making choices. Heather chose to make the bus turquoise blue and grey, because those colors contrasted well with the palette she wanted to use for the hills and the sky. Even if she had known that the Percival bus should have been cream and maroon, she might have chosen not to use the corporate colors because the cool colors she used make the bus stand out from the warm background.

Seeing only the rear end of the bus, coupled with its moving off to the left, suggests that it is leaving, just as seeing only the front end would have suggested arrival. By using little tricks like this you can reduce the amount of unnecessary detail you put into a rug, leaving plenty of room for the things that are more important to the story you tell.

The purple of the hills is reflected in the back of the bus. This is very subtle, but it suggests that Eleanor May, Peter and Keith are taking away with them a stack of wonderful memories and the promise of return visits.

Heather has used a simple technique to enhance the distinction between adjacent areas near the top of the rug. An almost solid dark line defines the horizon. Above it Heather has hooked straight slanting lines for the sunset-filled sky dipping away to the west, while below it flowing curved lines create the slopes of the heather-covered hills. This contrast in direction heightens the difference between areas whose colors are similar in tone.

The light of the setting sun, which has picked up some color from the heather-covered hills, is reflected in the back of the bus.

The hills meet the sky, and curved lines of hooking change to straight lines.

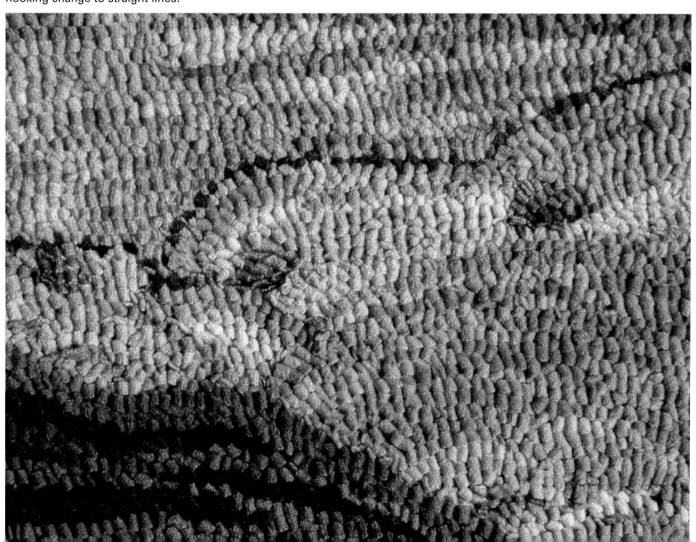

Eleanor May, heavily pregnant, sits opposite her two sons as they leave Swaledale to return to Sunderland.

Dyeing

Heather prefers to use "acid" dyes that are potentially dangerous in the powder form in which you buy them. When she gets a new powder, Heather mixes up a quantity of liquid dye following the instructions carefully: while doing so, she wears protective gloves and a face mask (to protect her eyes and prevent her breathing in the powder). The liquid is much safer to use because there is no loose powder to get into the air, although you must still wear gloves and old clothing and protect working surfaces from splashes. It is essential that you keep a set of utensils specifically for use when dyeing fabrics. Heather has an old enamel pan of her grandmother's that she loves to use for the memories associated with it. Heather covers the table she is working on with an oil cloth, and she covers that with a white plastic bag (an opened-out bin liner for instance) so that she can clearly see the colors she is producing.

The dyes Heather uses are called "acid" because you add acid (normally in the form of distilled/ white vinegar) to the dye. It is important to correctly prepare the fabric that is to be dyed. It must be pre-washed and, if you have not already done so, cut into manageable pieces before overnight soaking.

Make up the soaking solution in a plastic bucket and add a cup of vinegar to the water with a few drops of detergent — dish- or clothes-washing liquid is fine — before adding the fabric, making sure that every piece is under water. The vinegar is a mordant which makes the dye take and the detergent makes the fibers more porous so the fabric absorbs the dye better.

Acid dyes are effective on wool and silk as well as nylon (like tights or stockings), and Heather loves to use them to dye fleece as well as new flannel cloth. She enjoys playing (as she calls it) with the dyes on a variety of fabrics, including over-dyeing tweeds and kilts. Heather relishes the excitement of dyeing, the fact that you can seldom be sure what the final result will be until the fabric has dried. Her washing line after a dyeing session is a joy to behold, with multi-colored swatches of fabric and hanks of fleece blowing in the wind.

There are many types of dye on the market, and they each have their own method of use. Again, Heather's old friends trial and error will help you to find a dyeing technique that suits you — just take care with your health and safety as you have fun experimenting.

As is natural in a dales' scene, the road is separated from the fields by a stone wall. Heather really enjoys putting walls into her rugs; she says, "I love the colors and the ruggedness, the highlights. Tweeds are fabulous for stone walls." Peering over the top of this wall are three Swaledale sheep with their distinctive, almost circular, horns. Swaledales are very hardy sheep with deliciously curly coats keeping them warm, even in the coldest weather. These three would have been shorn in June or July, yielding the fleece Heather loves to include, both natural and dyed, in many of her rugs. Ironically, there is no fleece in *Percival's Bus*.

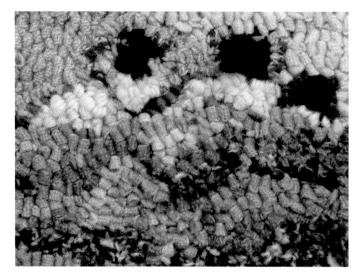

Swaledale sheep with their distinctive curly horns, look over the top of a dry stone wall.

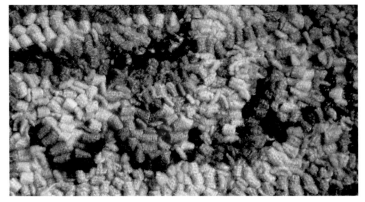

Pastel-colored flowers bloom on the grassy verge beneath the dry stone wall.

Tall spikes of flowers bloom alongside the road from Reeth to Richmond.

The jumbled browns and creams of the stone wall contrast beautifully with the pastel shades of the spikes of flowers growing in front of it, colors that are echoed in the blooms on the roadside verge nearest to us. Heather used mauve, but not purple, for these flowers — she reserved purple for the heather-covered hillsides. The mauve, pink and pale yellow flowers do not precisely represent any of the species that set the meadows of Swaledale ablaze with color in June and July. The hay harvested from the valley-bottom fields is sweet with blossoms of knapweed, buttercup, hawksbit and crane's-bill, among many others. Heather has captured some of that rich diversity in these few loops of colored wool — it is the jizz of the flowers that you see here.

Flowers in a Swaledale meadow just before the hay is cut.

The gate, depicted very simply in three shades of brown, is a good illustration of the importance of knowing where the light is coming from when you put something into a picture. In the bold lines of the sky, Heather has already identified that the light is coming from the west. She brought her watercolor painter's eye to this part of the scene: the upper surface of each piece of wood is light and the lower surface is dark. Out of four horizontal lines, two vertical lines and one strong diagonal, Heather has created a sturdy gate to keep the sheep from straying onto the road.

The five-bar gate which keeps the sheep in their field.

Dip dyeing

Heather dip-dyed the strips she used in the sky and the hills of *Percival's Bus*. Dip dyeing enables a variety of shades of the same color to appear in one cut strip of fabric. Many of the rugs in this book include dip-dyed flannel, showing how much Heather enjoys making use of this simple technique.

To produce the glorious breadth of shades she has used in this area of *Percival's Bus* (see below), Heather had a container of simmering water to which she added liquid dye mixture. The exact quantity of dye depends on the color to be produced, and it is important always to follow the instructions carefully.

With her bucket of soaked flannel to hand, Heather was ready to work on one piece of fabric at a time. First, she squeezed out most of the water. Then, holding the piece of fabric in tongs for safety, she immersed almost the whole of it into the dye bath before pulling it completely out of the liquid. She kept moving the fabric up and down, in and out of the dye, immersing a little less fabric in the liquid each time, to produce a progressively stronger color towards the bottom of the piece. It is important to keep the fabric moving to prevent a sharp dividing line appearing between shades. Heather might have dyed the piece square-on to the dye bath, but she might just as easily have chosen to suspend it by a corner.

Once Heather was happy with the shades in each piece (remembering that colors look darker when wet, although you can judge the range of shades you have obtained), she dropped it into another pan of simmering water and left it there for at least 20 minutes to "cook". This part of the process is vital with acid dyes — the fabric takes the dye up from the bath but the color must be fixed with heat. As will be explained for spot and casserole dyeing, there are several methods of cooking the fabric, and simmering in a pan of water is only suitable for pieces that have been dip-dyed. You can add more pieces of fabric to the pan as you work if it is big enough: start your timer when you add the last piece, then leave the whole lot to cook at a simmer for 20 minutes.

Whichever technique you use, you must rinse the fabric when the dye has been cooked into it. Use warm water to avoid stiffening the fabric by sudden cooling.

As this area of the sky in *Percival's Bus* shows, one dye bath can produce a wide variety of shades ranging from light to quite dark. Heather cut all the strips from one dye bath at the same time and made sure she cut them in a direction that ran through the progression of colors as well as along the grain of the fabric. She let all the strips from one dye bath mingle in the same basket so that when she dipped her hand in to pick up a strip, whatever its coloring, it would tone perfectly with its neighbors and add variety to the area in which she was working without any jarring clashes of color.

This small section of sky shows the wide range of colors obtained by dip dyeing.

The bus is just as simply and clearly defined, but it includes a level of detail that simply does not exist in a gate, like the wheel. Between the spokes we catch glimpses of the roadside flowers and the grassy verge as well as reflections of the setting sun. The dark rubber of the tire makes a clean curve against the blue paint of the wheel arch above it. Heather does not use black wool here — she tries to avoid black, preferring to use dark blues, browns and purples for the richness they bring to an area of darkness. (See *Guiding Light,* Chapter 7, for a good example of darkness that is not black.)

"This is me, this is the sort of work I love doing," Heather says. She has portrayed more modern subjects but says that she does not get the same feeling of joy in their creation that she gets from traditional work. "I can do it, but my heart's not in it," she explains.

Heather's heart is in *Percival's Bus* because it was such an important part of her childhood. "As a little girl I used to come up to the dale to stay on a farm in Hudswell. My dad would put me on the Darlington bus in Sunderland and when we got to Darlington the driver would make sure I got on the right bus to Richmond. Getting on that bus was amazing, everyone was shouting! They were shouting from the back of the bus to the front of the bus; they were shouting about what they had paid for things and what they had sold; everyone knew everyone else, and everyone knew everyone's business. I used to think I was in another world because in Sunderland nobody spoke to anyone else on the bus. In Yorkshire everyone shouted; I don't know whether I shout now." (There is more about those stays in Hudswell in Chapter 8, *Scarcote*.)

The reverse of *Percival's Bus* shows how densely Heather packs in the fabric. In the area surrounding the passengers virtually no backing is visible between the loops made with the same fabric. You can see small areas of backing where both the fabric and the direction of the hooking change at the same time. Sometimes when Heather filled in an area using more than one color she left a tiny sliver of backing uncovered, because it was too narrow for the even-sized strips she used throughout the work. This rug is made entirely with hooky and, naturally, Heather hooked the outline of the bus first. After creating the shape of the walls, gate, sheep, hills and horizon, she put the passengers into the bus before filling in the areas between those elements, including putting the grass-covered hillside in between the people.

With the exception of *The Steps* (Chapter 10), the rugs that appear in this book are all protected from wear because they hang on the wall. There are many lovely rugs which do lie on the floor of Heather's beautiful North Yorkshire home and, as far as Heather

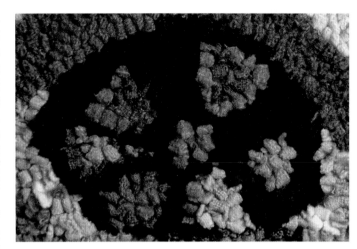

The wheel of the bus.

The other passengers, front of rug.

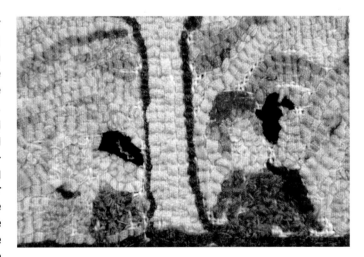

The other passengers (and the boys), reverse of rug.

is concerned, except in the finishing process, there is no fundamental difference in approach or technique in making a rug to hang on a wall or one that will lie on a floor.

Finishing off: edging and hanging

Heather enjoys finishing-off less than the creative part of rug-making, so she has evolved a process which ensures that this sequence of necessary tasks is completed efficiently and properly in as short a time as possible. Her aim is to enhance the design while protecting the reverse and edges from wear.

People occasionally ask Heather what kind of glue she uses to finish off her work, and her answer surprises most enquirers: "None." She explains that, if a rug is properly constructed on top-quality backing, it will hold together through the mechanical action of the strips pressing one against the other. Glue is simply not needed with a well-made rug, and this is another reason why it is important to use the best backing material you can obtain.

Heather explains that, historically, the only situation in which glue would be appropriate would be to waterproof a rug for use on a damp floor. In the bad old days when house floors were often flagstone laid straight onto the earth, an even coating of a rubbery glue spread across the entire reverse of the finished rug would help to prevent the pile getting damp. Rug-makers of old would also add an extra layer of backing to keep the reverse of the pile out of direct contact with the damp floor. This extra layer of hessian could be changed easily, much more quickly than making a new rug to replace one damaged by dampness.

Heather hooked *Percival's Bus* on white linen and, unusually for one of her rugs, it does not have whip-stitching around its edges. This is possible because the soft linen backing fabric folds over very easily, tight against the hooky work, unlike the more resistant and slightly brittle hessian. A rug that is made on a hessian backing normally has a few bare threads around its edges that need to be protected from wear by being whipped with yarn.

With a proddy rug there is less need to whip-stitch the edges, because the floppy strips of proddy work hang over the edge of the rug and protect the tiny raw edge, maybe three threads wide, that cannot be worked. Even with a floor rug, this edge is protected from wear because the physical bulk of the proddy strips on the reverse keeps the edge slightly above ground level.

Heather seldom imposes hard and fast rules, she normally gives advice; her suggestion is that you hook through one layer of backing right up to the edge of your design. When your work is complete, she suggests that you fold the raw edge over and cover it with sewn-on carpet tape.

Some people work in quite a different way, hemming the raw edge of the hessian before they start work and folding the edge over so that the hemming is two inches (5cm) in from the edge of the rug. They then work their hooky through these multiple layers, getting as close to the edge as they can and either leaving a narrow folded-over hessian edge or whipping around it with yarn.

In Heather's opinion, this method of working can produce problems, especially in floor rugs and with fine-worked hanging rugs. The hemmed edge produces a ridge of extra-thick backing and results in lumps forming in the corners. These are points that will wear if the rug is walked on and that look unsightly in a finely-detailed wall rug. Her dislike of this method is also partly based on the fact that she finds it hard on her hands to work through two or more layers of backing fabric.

Under the tape on the reverse of this rug, as with all of Heather's rugs, a single layer of backing fabric has a raw edge. She has mitred the corners of the backing fabric neatly by folding a triangle across the corner before covering all of the edges with carpet tape. Heather prefers not to trim away too much of the excess backing fabric from the sides or the corners of a rug, saying that "you cannot put back what you cut off."

You can use a needle and a length of yarn to whip-stitch all round the rug or you can crochet along the edge. Crochet is Heather's preferred technique and it produces a very neat and hard-wearing edge. Heather uses a rug hook rather than a conventional crochet hook as it puts less strain on her hands and fingers.

A floor rug may need a backing of strong fabric to protect the reverse of the loops from a rough floor. If you sew this to the carpet tape around the edge you will reduce the chance of the rug being pulled out of shape.

A wall rug needs something to hang by or from. This can be visible or invisible and, if visible, you can make the rod itself part of the design, as Heather has done with a small rug that depicts the incoming tide on the sea shore. Here the hanging rod is a piece of driftwood that is caught up in the net at the top of the rug, and it is a very effective design element.

There are various methods of hanging rugs. Heather's preferred method is to use a rod pushed through a sleeve that runs across the top edge of the rug. She usually creates this sleeve from a length of carpet tape, sewing it in a slightly tented shape to allow the rod to be slipped inside easily. After cutting the tape to length (slightly shorter than the rug's width), turn the ends over and slip-stitch them down. (If you do not sew the ends, the rod is likely to catch the tape rather than exit cleanly from the tunnel.) Sew the length of tape to the tape already

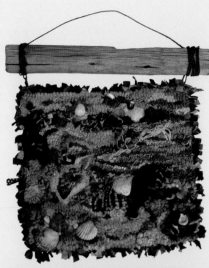

This rug, *Incoming Tide*, mixed media on even-weave Scottish hessian, 2006, 18 x 20 inches (45 x 50cm), makes a feature of its hanging rod by using it as part of the design.

Left to right, top to bottom: slip-stitching the edge; adding a crochet edge; laying the carpet tape in place to cover the raw edge; sewing the carpet tape in place with Aunt Jessie's thimble (optional!); a neatly-edged rug which Heather calls *Three Houses and Three Babies*; a mitred corner, flat and tidy, from *Bolton Castle*.

A neat round dowel forms a hanging rod: it is slipped inside a sleeve attached to the carpet tape at the top of the rug.

in place on the back of the rug, then cut your rod to length. You can hide the ends of the rod behind the corners of the rug.

Alternatively, you can make the rod a design feature. If you leave the ends of the rod sticking out of the sleeve, you can add tassels or other decoration, but remember that the rod has to fit through the sleeve so do not fix the trimmings until you have slid it into place.

You could use fabric tabs (such as are often seen on curtains) to hold the rod that supports the rug. These could be extensions of the rug or be made of a toning/contrasting fabric, as suits your design.

What all these methods have in common is a rod across the full width of the rug. This rod is vital: it ensures that your work is kept flat by keeping the weight of the rug evenly distributed and it protects any areas from excessive wear caused by supporting the weight. This is especially important if your rug is in an area where it might be brushed against by people passing it or if it is likely to be removed and re-hung regularly.

If you are hanging a rug from a wooden surface, cup hooks are usually adequate. If you are hanging a rug on a plastered wall, it is important to make sure that the hangers you use are up to the task of supporting the weight of your rug; a local picture framer should be able to sell you something appropriate. It is worth investing a little time getting the right hooks and hanging your rug properly; doing so could prevent damaging the wall if the weight of the rug pulled the hooks out of the plaster.

Heather uses perfectly ordinary carpet tape to cover the raw edge of the backing, slip stitching it in place with a toning cotton thread. She loves doing this hand sewing as it gives her an opportunity to use her aunt Jessie's thimble.

For a piece of Heather's hooky work this rug is unusual because the edges are not covered. Whip-stitching the exposed edge of backing fabric is not one of Heather's favorite tasks, but doing that job well finishes a rug off beautifully so she does it with as much enthusiasm as she can muster. Because she finds the crochet method easier and quicker, most of her recent rugs are finished this way. Sometimes Heather uses a mono-colored yarn which tones with the subject matter and sometimes she uses a yarn that is multi-colored. She usually does not know how she will finish a rug until the hooking is complete, preferring to let the completed rug dictate the method and materials she will use.

The backing of this rug is white linen which, combined with the wool loops, will ensure that it lasts for a very long time. But unless Heather breaks her habit and starts to write the story of each rug on a label on its reverse, they will last long after their meaning has been lost to future owners. Whatever happens, the quality of the materials and the clear work mean that Heather's descendants will be able to tell that the bus operated by Percival's was important to her. "I'll not leave any money," she said, "but I'll leave a rich inheritance of rugs — they will probably all be sold on eBay!"

7

Guiding Light

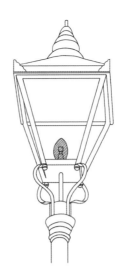

The memory Heather attaches to this rug is very precious to her and, even after sixty years, talking about it makes her very emotional. The focus of the rug is Heather's father, Victor, and creating the rug enabled her to tell part of the story of his life through one event. Because the story behind that event had a major impact on Heather's life, it is told in some detail.

Heather's father, Victor Robson, was born in Southwick, Sunderland, in 1897. He was 17 at the outbreak of WWI and enlisted in the Royal Marine Light Infantry. Before he went away to fight, he told his fiancée, Ethel Baker, from Barnard Castle, that he would marry her if he survived the war, but she was already very ill with tuberculosis when he returned. They eventually married in 1924 and were apparently only able to spend one year together before she died.

Understandably, it took Victor some time to recover from this loss and it was not until he was 36 that he felt able to marry again. He met his second bride, Heather's mother Eleanor May Milburn (seen below in a photo taken on their honeymoon in Edinburgh), when he was working as a pianist at the Sunderland Empire theatre and she was singing in a production of *Iolanthe* there. Eleanor May, who Heather describes as "a wonderful singer," was six years younger than Victor and their two sons, Peter and Keith, were born within five years of their wedding in 1933.

The only living creatures depicted in this rug are the eye-catching figures that represent Heather and her father, Victor. Heather made them using colors that do not appear in the rest of the rug. As a result,

Victor and Eleanor May Milburn on honeymoon in Edinburgh, Scotland, 1933. *Archives of the artist*

Heather, dressed in bright pink, holds her blind father's hand as they walk around the Grangetown area of Sunderland in the early 1950s.

Guiding Light, fine-cut wool on white linen, 1999. 32 x 15 inches (81 x 38cm). *Collection of the artist*

the young Heather stands out like a beacon, a guiding light in pink, although the adult Heather denies that there was any conscious thought behind that. She said, "I dyed the other fabrics I used specially for this rug, but I made the figures using strips I had in my bit box. The little girl comes to the fore because she is a warm color, cool colors recede. I wasn't thinking about what I was doing by making the little girl the main thing that stands out from the background." Victor's tweedy coat and hat are a beautiful mixture of rich browns and the shading on his arm, bent to hold Heather's hand, is perfectly executed.

Victor was a talented, self-taught musician and composer. He accompanied silent films at the Sunderland Empire Palace (as it was originally known), which opened in 1907 and is still the largest theatre in the area between Leeds and Glasgow. He also played piano at the Savoy Theatre in Southwick, Sunderland, and taught singing and the piano at home. "There was a great big brass plaque on the front of our house in Grangetown which read 'Teacher of Pianoforte and Singing'," said Heather. She remembers that her father had a lovely singing voice.

Some silent films were delivered to the cinema with musical scores for the pianist to play from, but many were not. As well as sight-reading the scores, Victor would have been called upon to improvise pieces to match the mood of the action. He always took his dog, Jack, to work with him, and Jack was very popular with the cinema audiences. This clever little dog would appear to laugh or cry at the on-screen action in sympathy with Victor's playing, and he would beg for food at the ends of the rows of seats. Victor and Jack were inseparable. After Eleanor May and the boys were evacuated from Sunderland to Langthwaite in 1939 (see Chapter 5, *The Evacuees*) and bombs started to fall, "Jack went mad with the noise," to use Heather's phrase. He became so distressed that Victor had no choice but to ask the vet to put him to sleep. Victor never got over the fact that (as he saw it) he had murdered his faithful dog. At that time he could never have foreseen that his feelings surrounding the death of a much-loved pet and friend would have a significant impact on his life in the future.

Victor and his faithful dog Jack. *Archives of the artist.*

Even as a soldier in WWI, Victor's eyesight had been poor. His vision deteriorated as he got older but it did not stop him earning a living. His work as a cinema pianist was dramatically reduced when the talkies arrived in the 1930s. When that major change affected his income, Victor took a job as an insurance salesman for the Liverpool Victoria Society in Sunderland. His work as a teacher of piano playing and singing was unaffected by his sight problems because of the essentially aural nature of the task. His voluntary war-time work as a fire marshal continued, despite his failing sight, because his vision was still good enough to keep watch in the darkness for the bright fires that were started by incendiary bombs.

During the war, the street lights were turned off, but a dominant feature of this rug is the gas-lamp lighting Heather's way as she walks through the streets of Grangetown, Sunderland, with her father. Gas-lamps hissed when they illuminated the streets at night and Heather commented, "I feel ancient talking about gas-lamps, but that's what we had when I was a little girl."

By the time WWII ended in 1945 Victor had lost the sight of one eye completely and the sight he had in the other eye was deteriorating fast. Heather remembers the limitations of his vision when she was a tiny girl. "He could tell black from white, he could see shadows, and he knew the sun was shining but that was all."

In this rug the colors of the moon and the dramatic clouds surrounding it suggest that Heather and her father are walking at night in the depths of winter. She has used the same purples and creams

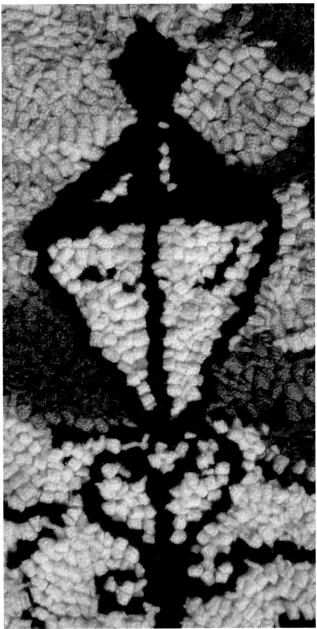

The gas-lamp lights Heather's way, but Victor can only hear it.

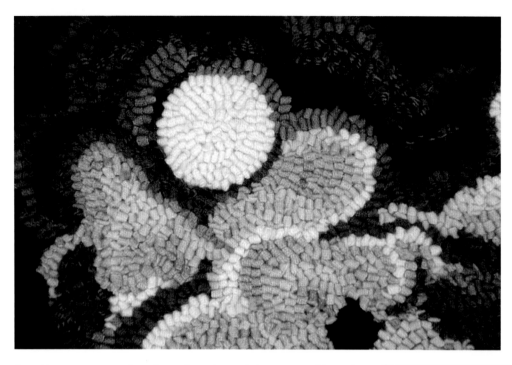

The moon peeps out from behind the clouds, lighting their edges against the dark sky.

for the moon, clouds, street and houses, thereby deliberately keeping the palette of colors fairly narrow. Heather describes the rug as "playing with colors." She wanted it to be night-time because she loves the colors of dark skies and she needed it to be a dark scene so she could create the effect of light from the street lamp. The sky is not black — Heather seldom uses black in a rug — but it is a rich mixture of shades of purple. Coupled with the directional hooking Heather uses to great effect throughout this rug, these colors give a depth and intensity to the sky that flat black hooky could not produce.

The moon illuminates the clouds that tower above the houses. All the buildings are three or four stories high but they are not intended to represent a real location and you will not find this street anywhere in Sunderland. Heather is so familiar with Sunderland that she was able to create a fictitious street from a collection of memories and mental images. It closely resembles those parts of Sunderland's East End that suffered major bomb damage during the war and have since been demolished.

The Robson family home in Sunderland was near the Eye Infirmary, and it was to that hospital that Victor was sent when he finally sought medical advice about his one good eye in 1950. He was offered an operation which might improve his sight and he decided to go through with it, despite the fifty-percent risk that his remaining vision might be destroyed.

At that time, hospitals were much less welcoming places than they are now and children were barred from the wards unless they were the patient. Heather and her brothers were not allowed to visit their father during his 14-week stay in hospital. To prevent his retina moving before the wound was fully healed, Victor was strapped

The gas-lamp illuminates the nearest edge of this building, while all of the windows glow with light from inside.

Victor's clock now has pride of place in Heather's home: he wore away the numbers on the face as he felt for the time.

to the bed and told to keep perfectly still. The eye that had been operated on was covered with a dressing, leaving his blind eye uncovered, so Victor was unable to see anything or do anything for himself. Heather remembers being smuggled up the iron steps of a fire escape outside his ward to see him, "when the nice nurse was on duty instead of the awful sister." She has a vivid memory of what she saw. "Dad was lying on his back in bed and a nurse was feeding him liquid from a china pot with a spout on it."

When the bandages were removed, Victor realized that the operation had failed and he was completely blind. He took this devastating blow in his stride and decided to learn how to cope without sight. Heather remembers walking home from the hospital with her father, a walk that lasted about ten minutes. When they reached the family bungalow, Victor asked his family, kindly but firmly, to let him walk the last few steps alone. He said that he had to become independent and that included being able to get around by himself. Heather, her mother and her brothers all watched nervously as Victor walked the short distance from the gate to the front door by himself.

The clock shown above now has pride of place on the mantelpiece above the open fire in Heather's home. It was Victor's clock, and he used it to tell the time in two ways after he lost his sight. It chimes the hours, so he could tell the passing time by ear. He would also open the glass front and put his hands on the face to feel the position of the clock's hands. You can see how the dial has been worn by the pressure of his needing to know the time. Heather is delighted to have this lovely clock to remind her of her father every time she looks at it. Victor also had a Braille watch and bedside clock and, through Rug Aid, Heather was able to give one of the older blind rug-making trainees at the GOVI center in The Gambia a Braille watch. The new owner very proudly shows it to every visitor to the workshop. (You can see a photo of him at www. rug-aid.org and you can read more about Rug Aid in Chapter 18, *Origins and Identity*).

This rug is made entirely of wool. Heather dip dyed white flannel to produce the breadth of shades of purple she needed for the shadows and the dark sky. The windows are bright yellows, creams and whites to represent the light and life within the buildings.

Despite stressing how important it is to draw the basic elements of your design onto the backing before you start work, Heather is keen to emphasise that you should only use the lines as a guide. "You can hook over the lines until it looks right," she says. "Here I have used directional hooking to make the swirly patterns in the dark sky and I have used straight rows for the buildings and the paths. Despite the sad story, this was a fun rug to create and it was lovely to work on. It was made extra special because I love these dark colors and the story the rug tells is a very significant part of my life." The straight rows have a very clear vanishing point and the perspective of this rug is very striking. It is hard to resist wondering what is around the corner to the right.

Choosing and preparing backing fabrics

Heather feels frustrated when she sees students making beautiful rugs on poor-quality backings; such people are making life more difficult for themselves because of the uneven weave of the backing and its inherent weakness.

Heather's preferred backing is linen (second and third from bottom in photo) for its hard-wearing nature and wonderful softness, but linen is too expensive to use all the time. She has used monk's cloth (bottom of pile) and other evenly woven, open-textured fabrics as well as plastic sacking. Plastic sacking, when used with a plastic pile such as recycled carrier bags, is ideal where the finished rug will become wet, like outdoor garlands or in bathrooms.

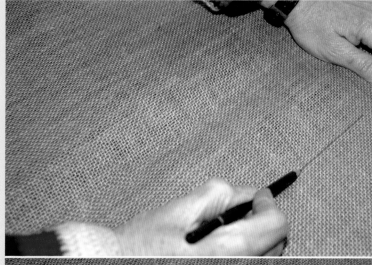

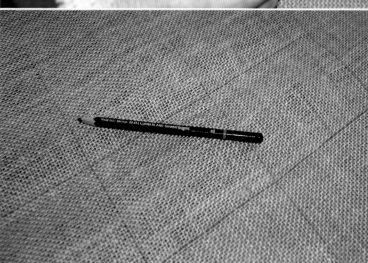

Top to bottom: even-weave Scottish hessian; even, closely-woven woollen cloth; open-weave woollen cloth; white linen; natural linen; monk's cloth.

Heather made her earliest rugs using a backing of old hessian sacks. She still uses hessian regularly but she does not use old sacks any longer, except in The Gambia (see Chapter 18, *Origins and Identity*).

Today Heather buys an even-weave hessian direct from the mill in Scotland (top of pile in photo). She explains that the uneven weave of the cheap hessian used for sacks makes it unsuitable for the fine pictorial work for which she is known.

There are some stiff moulded plastic backings available, but Heather is not a big fan of them. "They have their uses," she says, "but they are not appropriate for a memory rug."

Getting the grain of your backing straight before you cut it makes it easier to work on and, if you use good backing fabric, it takes but a moment's preparation to get the grain straight. Wherever possible, Heather uses top-quality fabric with an even weave. As a result she can be sure that, if she runs the point of her soft pencil along the "ditch" between the threads, she will automatically draw a dead straight line to cut along. She uses this technique to mark the cutting lines for her backing, measuring and marking the size from the selvedge and drawing a straight pencil line between the points she has marked without using a ruler, to make sure the grain is straight before starting to cut the backing.

Heather has noticed to her disappointment that pre-printed patterns are sometimes supplied with the printing slightly off the straight grain which, as she observes, makes it very difficult to create a straight line as part of the design.

Whatever type of backing you use, allow a four-inch (10cm) margin all round to turn in when your design is complete and mark the boundary of your work area before you start to transfer the design to the backing. To stop the edge of your backing fraying as you work on it, you can either bind the raw edge of your backing with adhesive tape (masking tape is good for this purpose) or machine-sew the edge with a complex stitch which will hold the threads together.

Heather uses a very soft pencil, usually 4B, without a ruler to draw straight line on the backing by following the weaving lines.

Soon after losing his sight, Victor was offered a guide dog as a mobility aid but, remembering Jack and the trauma of having to end his life, he rejected the idea. He said, "I cannot go through that again as long as I live" and, reaching out for Heather's hand, he added "I've got my little guide dog here." He devised a scheme in which, with his five year-old daughter Heather holding his hand, he would learn a mental route map of the neighbourhood.

And that is the story behind the rug *Guiding Light*, how Heather was given the task of walking the streets of Grangetown holding Victor's hand until he felt confident to walk them alone. As they walked, she would describe what she could see and they would count the steps it took Victor to reach the street corner or to get from curb to curb across the road. Victor's mental map grew in detail and extent until he felt safe to move about on his own throughout quite a large radius from home. "Eventually he was able to get to Garbutt's the bread shop and to Feller's. He would go into town to pay the bills," said Heather. "People could not believe how he always knew where he was. It was because we had done all those walks together." Heather continues, "I was born to be my dad's little guide dog. It must have been a shock to my mother to find she was having me at 44. Imagine her surprise when she found out she was pregnant again, but I am sure this is why I was born."

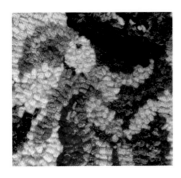

Heather's red pompom hat matches her red scarf, and she gazes loving at her father.

The tiny figure of Heather gazes up at her tall father as they emerge from a dark alley into the brightness of the moon- and gas-lit street. Holding hands, they walk towards the lamp-post on the corner. The warmth of the light the lamp casts onto their faces echoes the warmth of the love they felt for one another. This feeling was with them all the time but it was especially strong during these walks when Victor relied on his daughter to help him re-establish his place in society.

As they enter the gas-lamp's glow, father and daughter are walking on the smooth paving stones of the alley and, if they turn left, they will continue to walk on that even surface. Should they need to cross this street they will walk on the cobbles that formed the surface of so many of Sunderland's streets at the time. For a person with a visual impairment a cobbled street must be a challenging surface to negotiate safely, although the texture would have given Victor a welcome clue to his location. Hooky using dip dyed strips is ideal to represent the uneven surface of the cobbled street, as each slightly differently-shaded loop resembles one of the granite blocks.

Victor is wearing a hat, as most men did in 1950s Britain.

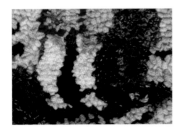

Heather is wearing yellow socks under her T-bar sandals and Victor is wearing stout dark shoes.

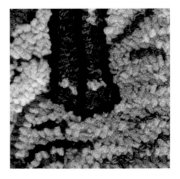

Many urban streets in Britain were still paved with hard-wearing cobbles in the 1950s.

Moving ahead almost sixty years, Heather remembers something that happened when she was in The Gambia in 2007. "Sausie [one of the blind trainees at the GOVI center — see Chapter 18, *Origins and Identity*] was in class with his little girl and he said 'she's my sight.' The first thing she says to him every day is 'Daddy, what can I get for you, what do you want?' That could have been me speaking because that is what I would always say to my father. Sausie's daughter's experience and mine are exactly the same, even though they happened in different worlds and different lives."

Sausie and his daughter at the Rug Aid workshop in The Gambia. Sausie is blind and his daughter is his Guiding Light. *Courtesy of Mat Connolley/Rug Aid cic*

8

Scarcote

This is one of the most symbolic of Heather's memory rugs. It was being finished while this book was being written, as you can see by the tiny threads of linen backing that are visible in some of the photos. *Scarcote* is also one of Heather's very successful attempts to reflect contemporary influences in her rug-making, as her children often encourage her to do. This beautiful rug loosely follows the rules governing the design of modern Azeri rugs, one of which is to use a palette of just three colors: Heather has chosen to combine red, green and gold (and closely related shades) with white and black for outlining. One of the tests of the balance of the design of an Azeri rug is to put your thumb down on the pile and rotate your hand around it. Your outstretched fingers should pass over all of the colors used in the rug, and *Scarcote* passes this test.

Azeri rugs are a form of Oriental rug that tell stories that usually reflect the lives of the people who make them. This rug relates some of the memories Heather associates with Scarcote, the farm near Hudswell that is central to the stories told in Chapters 5 and 18, *The Evacuees* and *Origins and Identity*.

The central area of an Azeri rug is called the field and the border is known as the band. The band of this rug uses a floral pattern that is Heather's interpretation of someone else's design. There are very few flowers in the field so she filled the band with them, carefully-spaced. She says that "the whole of Scarcote was full of wild flowers and that is why I gave this rug a floral border. I copied it from a book, but I cannot for the life of me remember which one." If it is your design, thank you: it sets this rug off beautifully.

The band's background is hooked in neat straight lines of shaded gold. To avoid having flat color, Heather dyed a batch of wool flannel and cut it into strips. She then "dumped" (to use her word) the strips into a basket and mixed them up. When she hooked the background of the band, she picked strips at random. The resulting rich variety of shades adds life and interest to an otherwise plain area.

Only three colors are used in this Azeri rug, shades of red, green and gold (plus white and black): all three appear in this owl and its perch in a tree.

The border features a simple repeated floral motif.

Scarcote, fine-cut wool on white linen, 2009. 45 x 31 inches (114 x 78cm). *Collection of the artist.*

Scarcote is a small house with attached outbuildings.

A fine black line, one strip wide, separates the band from the field simply and neatly. The field has a rich background of far-from-flat reds (dyed especially for this rug) and, in the same way as the band, the variously-shaded strips were picked at random from a basket. Heather made a deliberate decision not to make the field green, even though it represents one of the actual fields of Scarcote. This was part of her need to think differently about rug-making, an attitude that was so important in this rug.

But Heather did not start either of those backgrounds until she had completed the elements they contain, thereby following her preferred reverse-watercolor technique (as outlined in Chapter 3, *The Ha'penny Ferry*). Although there is some directional hooking in this rug, you can see straight lines in many of the design's elements (like the tent and the trees). Heather believes that Canadian rug-hookers were the first to emulate the Azeri style: the Canadian rug-hooking style called Grenfell follows straight lines that emulate the rows of yarn in a woven rug.

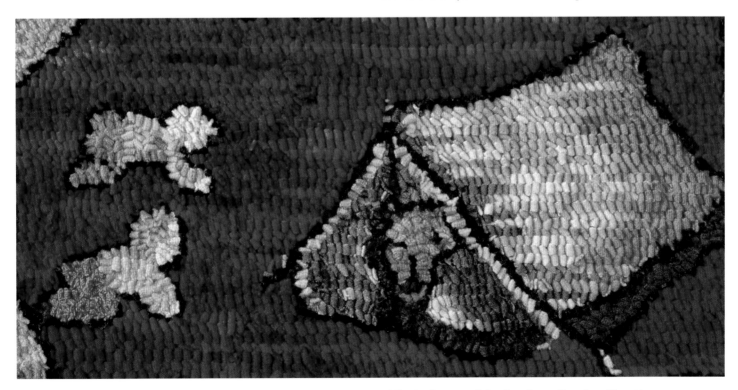

The side of the tent and the background show clear straight lines while the boys and the fox show directional hooking.

Scarcote is a very isolated building. Naturally, Heather remembers the trees behind the house – that's where the owls sat and hooted.

names of Swaledale are of very mixed origins with a lot of Viking, Norse and Saxon influences: the second half of the farm's name almost certainly comes from the Saxon word "cott," meaning a humble house (as in cottage). The first part probably refers to the farm's position: it is situated just south of the steep cliff (or "scar" in the Saxon meaning) alongside the road between Reeth and Richmond. Romantically-inclined readers may prefer it to derive from the name of the first, Saxon, farmer. In the case of the Yorkshire seaside town of Scarborough, Scar means that this was Skarthi's-borough: Skarthi means hare-lip, so Scarcote could mean "the farm belonging to the man with the hare-lip" (who probably died long before the end of the tenth century). That conjures up some wonderful and dramatic images.

Before relating some of the stories told in this rug, a little background information might help to set the scene. There was a settlement at Hudswell (the current village center is about a mile east of the farm) in 1086; we know this because Hudswell is mentioned in *The Domesday Book*, the two-volume survey commissioned by William the Conqueror to assess the taxes he could raise on the land and resources of his newly-acquired territory, England. In contrast, we know very little about Scarcote: it is probably nothing more than an old English farm and it does not appear to have any great or inherent architectural, social or historical merit. The place

By the time Heather's mother and brothers were evacuated to Scarcote at the outbreak of WWII, the farm was owned by the Beattie family. When Heather first met the Beatties, the matriarch was a woman known to everyone as Old Auntie Beattie. She had been christened Ada Margaret Hunt in about 1891 and her family had long been associated with Hudswell and nearby villages. Old Auntie Beattie would have been in her late fifties or early sixties when Heather met her, and she died in 1976.

When Old Auntie Beattie was still plain Ada Hunt, in about 1907, she married John Beattie. He had been born in Corbridge, just over the border in County Durham, in 1884. They had two sons and one daughter: John Frederick, always known as Fred, was born in 1908, Peggy in 1911, and, later, Reginald was born. The Beattie brothers married the Whittle sisters. Fred and Hilda lived on the farm with Old Auntie Beattie while Reg and Joan lived in the village of Hudswell. Old Auntie Beattie's husband John died in 1931 so her sons (and their wives) took on a lot of the farm work, although their mother retained an active role in life on the farm until the family retired from farming in 1960.

Joan and Reg Beattie spent their honeymoon in Sunderland, staying with Heather's parents at their Grangetown home. Heather remembers her mother telling her to stay away from the bedroom. "Me mam and dad must have given up their bed for Joan and Reg, though heaven knows where they slept," said Heather.

Peter (standing) and Keith (on his mother's knee) behind Scarcote with one of Auntie Beattie's older granddaughters and two of the Beatties' cattle. *Archives of the artist.*

Peggy was the first to get married: she and her husband lived in Hudswell and they had two daughters. Joan and Reg also had two daughters, Linda and Susan, who were much younger than Peggy's two. Heather said that their grandmother Beattie, Uncle Fred and Auntie Hilda worshipped the girls. Heather adored them too, and the three younger girls spent many happy hours together when Heather was in her mid-teens. She described her job as "keeping them out of harm's way because they were always getting into mischief" and said that they would walk for miles and she would make up endless stories for them. Linda and Susan spent at least one holiday in Sunderland with Heather and her parents, during which the girls saw the sea for the first time. In this rug, Linda and Susan are swinging on the farm gate, something Heather remembers the three of them being scolded for more than once.

Linda and Susan climb on the farm gate.

Scarcote farmhouse is obviously an old building and Heather remembers that all the bedrooms opened from one to the other in the manner known as passage rooms. It is likely that, when the house was first built, the bedroom at the top of the stairs would have been the largest one, used by the master and mistress of the household.

Heather said, "I don't know for sure why my mother and brothers were evacuated to Scarcote, but I think it might have been something to do with my dad's first wife, Ethel Baker. There was a Baker family in Hudswell and they were great friends of the Beattie family. The connection might have been something as simple as the Bakers saying to

The owls provided one of the memorable sounds Heather heard during nights at Scarcote.

my parents, 'we know someone with a farm in the country. Eleanor May and the boys could escape the bombing there.' After a while at Scarcote my mother and brothers moved to Brookside, a cottage in High Green, Langthwaite. She remained in contact with the Beatties and, when the war was over, we kept up that connection with Scarcote."

Sadly, much later, Joan and Reg Beattie were obliged to live in separate residential care homes in Richmond. Joan died in 2009 and Heather was reunited with her daughters, Linda and Susan, at Joan's funeral.

Heather tells a delightful story about going to bed at Scarcote:

> At Scarcote I heard owls for the first time in my life. They lived in the trees behind the house and I'd never heard anything like it at home in Sunderland. I'd carry my candle up to bed in a little tin and I'd see all the shadows on the walls as I was going up the stairs. I climbed up into the big old brass bed I shared with Old Auntie Beattie, snuggled down into the feather mattress, and watched the shadows cast on the walls and ceiling by the candle flame flickering on the table beside the bed. As I lay there, warm and safe, the trees behind the house would be moaning in the wind. I used to lie in bed with the candles, the shadows and the moans. Those are very strong memories, even after all this time.
>
> All the while the adults downstairs would think I was asleep but I'd be listening to their conversations. There were no carpets, you see, not even rugs, to muffle the sound coming through the cracks between the floorboards. That's all there was for the ceiling of the room below and I could hear every word they said. When I heard the sneck click on the door at the bottom of the stairs I'd know someone was coming up to bed so I'd quickly blow out the candle and snuggle down, pretending to be asleep.

In common with many old farmhouses that were normally only one room deep, there was a small dairy between the house and the byre where the cows were milked by hand. Swallows nested in the beams of the byre, and Heather has vivid memories of seeing Uncle Fred at work there. Fred, his head resting against the cow he is milking, is included in the rug. The white lines radiating from the cow's udder are why Heather has such strong memories of seeing this twice-daily event. She describes what is portrayed in the rug: "there I am, standing with my arms in the air. Uncle Fred would sit on the three-legged stool in the milking parlour next to the house, milking the cows by hand. I always tried to

A sneck: holding the handle, your thumb is perfectly placed to press the flat tongue at the top and raise the bar which holds the door shut.

sneak past without him noticing me but he would hear me coming. He would squirt me with milk and I got covered in it!"

The milk was cooled by being poured from the bucket over a water-cooled device a bit like a reverse radiator, and it was caught beneath this contraption in a ten-gallon aluminum milk churn. There are clear one gallon marks on the back of the example opposite. Every day those patient hand-milked cows filled two churns, several jugs for the farm's kitchen and, in the dairy, some wide bowls of cream-rich

Fred Beattie, sitting on a traditional three-legged milking stool, aims a squirt of milk at Heather.

milk for butter-making. Records show that British cows were producing about a gallon (eight pints at 20 fluid ounces per pint, roughly 4.5 litres) at each milking in the 1950s, so the Beatties probably had about ten cows. Each cow almost certainly had a pet name, and they would have been loved and treated like pets by the family.

Uncle Fred lifted both of the churns on to the farm's bogie (a small hand-made wooden cart on wheels) and Heather would help him to push it up the long track to the farm gate. As they walked, they would have been able to hear the sound of the milk sloshing around inside the churns. The animals were calling to each other, the dog was barking at everything that moved, and the birds were singing, but there were very few aeroplanes roaring through the sky and very little traffic on the local roads to drown out the low-level background noise.

"It was quite hilly up the banks," says Heather. "I would help Uncle Fred push the bogie to the gate then ride all the way back in the cart with the empty churns clanging into each other beside me as we went over the bumps. There were two churns to go to the gate every day after the morning milking and they were left there for the dairy lorry to collect them." You can see those two churns just beside the five-bar gate that bears the farm's name so proudly, and you can decide for yourself whether they are heavy, full of creamy

This aluminum milk churn has two small handles by which it could be lifted when empty and rolled on its base rim when full. *Courtesy of Ceredigion Museum, Aberystwyth*

Two milk churns by the roadside.

The Beatties, Reg (on the horse) and Joan (immediately behind the horse), Fred and Hilda, with Eleanor May (far right), Peter and Keith (on Fred's knee) on a sledge pulled along by Bessie. *Archives of the artist*

Peter, sitting on the grass, and Keith, standing on his mother's lap, enjoy a sunny day in a flowery meadow at Scarcote. *Archives of the artist*

Heather looks a little grumpy, despite her very smart coat, as she sits beside her mother outside The Red Lion in Langthwaite, Arkengarthdale, with some of Eleanor May's friends. The pub has hardly changed since this photo was taken in the early 1950s. *Archives of the artist*

cows' milk, or light and empty, awaiting the ride back to the farm on the bogie. The Milk Marketing Board (which carried out its work from 1933 to 1994) bought all the milk Britain's dairy farmers could produce for a guaranteed price, which made incomes from cow-keeping fairly predictable. Old Auntie Beattie, Fred and Reg must have welcomed the regular payments that the milk brought to the farm.

Heather's mother, Eleanor May, and her brothers "turned up" (to use Heather's phrase) at Scarcote at the very beginning of WWII. At the same time, Eleanor May's next door neighbor from Sunderland, Mrs. Jones, was also evacuated to Scarcote with her two young sons, Alan and Howard. There is no way of knowing how this apparent coincidence came about. It would be less remarkable for neighbors to be evacuated to the same place if the evacuation was a formal part of Operation Pied Piper, but Heather thinks that her mother made her own arrangements. Perhaps Mrs. Jones was related to the Beattie family and was the driving force. It is too late now to ask any of the adults involved, and the children who were evacuated with them would only rarely have known why they went where they did. In the mid-20th century, and especially at times of great stress like war, children were consulted much less about their lives and futures than is the case now.

Heather acknowledges that life for the Beatties must have changed dramatically when the two women and four boys arrived at Scarcote from Sunderland. She said, "I don't know how they put up with it. It must have been a terrible shock to the system. It was only a little three or four bedroom cottage, and the bedrooms led from one to the next." In fact, the Beatties did not have to "put up with it" for very long. Like quite a lot of evacuated families, Mrs. Jones and her two boys returned to Sunderland fairly quickly as the phoney war unfolded in the period from September 1939 to April 1940, and the massive bombing campaigns which had been predicted failed to materialise straight away. And, after staying at Scarcote for a little while, Heather's mother and brothers moved to a cottage in Langthwaite, so the Beatties got their house back.

Nevertheless, strong bonds had been forged between the Robson and Beattie families. After the 1944 D-Day operation, which started the liberation of France and weakened the Nazis' hold on Europe, Heather's mother and brothers (plus the daughter/sister who would be born that November) returned to Sunderland. They took with them a standing invitation to visit Scarcote for their holidays. With little money coming in after Heather's father, Victor, lost his sight, this was a welcome offer and they took it up as often as they could. Heather said that she spent every Easter and summer holiday from school at Scarcote until she was 16. "The only holiday I never came up was

Christmas." At that time (1960), although the Beatties sold the farm and retired, the two families stayed in touch.

"The farm was abandoned to the army because they owned all of the land around it," Heather says. "Les and I tried to buy it at one time but we found out that the army never sells their land. Les still tells people that the farm belongs to the Queen of England, as she is the head of the army! It is such an awful shame that they used the farm buildings for target practice — the doors and windows were all shot to pieces when we went to visit. The farmer that lives two fields away has rented all the fields from the army and his son and family are in the house now. They have done it up and it's lived in, they have spent a lot of money on it." It is good to know that Scarcote is a family home again after all the fun Heather had there in the 1950s. She says that there were too many stories to put everything into the rug, but she has managed to incorporate quite a lot of them.

Heather describes how she got to Scarcote for her holidays:

Heather stands between her parents in the last photo which was taken before the operation which left Victor completely blind. *Archives of the artist*

> It was a magical little place, a mile up the road from Hudswell. It was all on its own in a little sheltered spot overlooking the Reeth road, surrounded by stone walls. As a child, going there for my holidays was just magic. I remember being eight years old and my dad putting me on a bus in Grangetown, Sunderland, to Darlington. He asked the driver 'Will you see she gets off in Darlington, and will you put her on the Richmond bus?' I had my little case and my little lunch with me, and the driver would look after me. I always sat behind him and he put me on the Richmond bus. When I got to Richmond there were Fred and Hilda Beattie waiting for me in their ex-Post Office van. They used to buy these old vans and they would hand-paint the name out but you could always see it peeping through. I was terrified because they put me in the back of the van and I'd look out of the windows in the rear doors. Tunstall Hill was the steepest in Sunderland, otherwise it was almost totally flat, and here I was surrounded by hills steeper than I'd ever seen. I was terrified of the doors opening as this rickety old van went up one of the hills. We'd drive up these banks and I was terrified, hanging on and thinking, 'Oh, those doors are going to open and I'll fall out!'

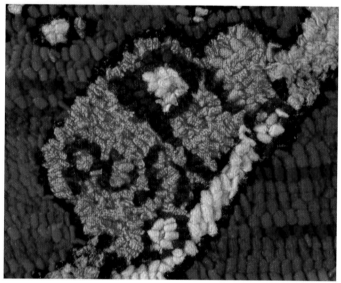

The Beattie's ex-Post Office van, with the word "POST" still visible through the paint that was applied to hide the letters, climbs the steep bank to Scarcote.

You can see the red van in the middle of the rug: it is clearly a Post Office van and the word "POST" is legible through the hand-applied paint. But it is not delivering post, it is delivering Heather and that is why she has shown the van going up a steep hill. The lane from the gate to the farmhouse was winding and hilly, as are most of the roads in Swaledale.

Alongside a clump of cowslips, three bottles of cowslip wine pop their corks.

Those roads pass between verges and hedgerows filled with wild flowers, just as the fields surrounding Scarcote were smothered in them. Among the very few flowers included in the field of this Azeri-style rug are some cowslips, just above the milk churns and alongside some bottles whose tops are exploding. Why? Heather explains:

> The fields were full of cowslips and every year we went out with baskets and picked them. Old Auntie Beattie would make them into cowslip wine. She kept the bottles in a great big old stone pantry next to the kitchen. It had stone shelves and stone slabs on the floor to keep everything cool, like milk and eggs and the butter she made to sell at market. One night we were woken up by what sounded like world war three. There was all this banging going on, and everyone was wondering what it was. We all crept downstairs and discovered that most of the bottles of cowslip wine had exploded. That's why they are next to the cowslips in the field.

Just above the noisy and dangerous wine is a sledge. This is based on a photo of Reg Beattie sitting on Bessie, a fine strong-looking horse that is pulling some members of the Robson and Beattie families through one of Scarcote's fields on a sledge. You will notice that there is no saddle so there are no stirrups and Reg is simply sitting on a blanket draped over Bessie's back. As Heather sat on top of a wobbly load of hay piled high on the wooden cart, the gentle steady rhythm produced by Bessie's sure-footed steps was in sharp contrast to the jerking motion produced by the tractor with which the Beatties replaced her.

Heather reversed the direction of the sledge in the photo so that it fitted into the available space.

Just in front of the rickety old fence that separates the two fields, Heather has included herself turning the hay. She said, "I have a handkerchief on my head to protect my red hair from the sun. I have the most wonderful memories of working for hours on end in the hay fields: my hands were blistered but I didn't mind." Heather and her co-worker are turning the hay with wooden rakes, just like the ones her parents are using in the fantastic photo below.

Back to that rickety old fence. Heather remembers that there were lots of fences like that on the farm, as well as hedges and walls. Just behind the fence is a dog kennel with a fierce-looking guard dog doing his job, standing up on his hind legs and barking, pulling on his chain, which is fastened to a stake in the ground. "He'd bark at everything and try to run after anything which moved, so he's barking at the van arriving," says Heather.

Eleanor May and Victor look too clean and tidy for this to be anything other than a staged photo, but it is a charming one all the same. *Archives of the artist*

The man behind Heather is wearing y-shaped braces as he works.

The dog's lead is fastened to a stake in the ground.

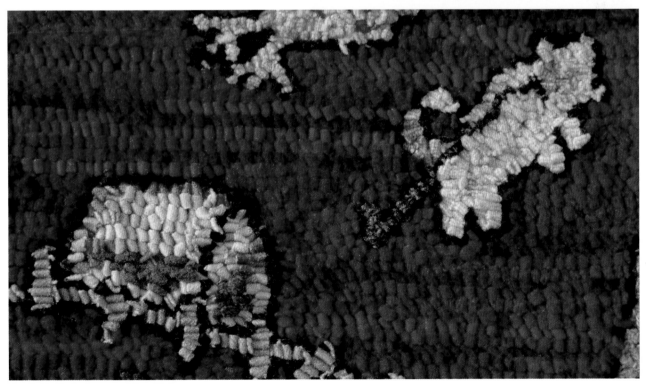

The bottom half of the stable door is firmly shut as Heather yells for Fred's protection from the cockerel – isn't he gorgeous?

Although the hinges are broken and two sheep use it as a bedroom, this two-seat earth closet in Fremington, only a mile from Reeth, is a very welcome and rare survival. *Courtesy of Mick and Jane Bell, Lionel and Lulu*

That van is bringing Heather for one of her regular holidays. Everything about Scarcote thrilled and delighted her except The Cockerel (just above the dog). He deserves those capital letters as he was, according to Heather, "the hugest, angriest, most horrible cockerel in the world."

Scarcote's facilities were primitive, as Heather explains:

I'm in the earth closet just to the left of the house and I am stuck there just like I was every morning, screaming for help with the bottom half of the stable door very firmly shut.

I'm stuck because that nasty cockerel would fly at the door and stop me coming out! I used to have to scream for help every day and Uncle Fred always came to rescue me. Eventually he wrung the cockerel's neck and I could use the earth closet in peace. There were three seats in a row, but I never shared with anyone… I do remember the feeling of the cold wind, and being afraid that a rat might bite me. There were always hens and chicks running around near the house, and the cockerel would terrify them too.

Some of the many hens and chicks.

As well as no indoor plumbing, there was no electricity at Scarcote. The hurricane lamp, just below the trees near the top of the rug, and the candle in the bedroom window remind us of that. "There was no running water, just a big tank sunk into the ground down the back field," says Heather. "It was filled with the pure clean water that flowed out of the hillside. One of my jobs every day was to carry water from the well (as we called it) to the boiler next to the range where it was heated up." Even with the simple life the Beatties led, Heather must have carried a great many heavy, sloppy, buckets over the years, but she would (nearly) always have had a willing heart and a wide smile as she went to and from the well.

The well is not depicted in the rug. Heather's choice of objects relating to Scarcote and their relative positions in the field is not supposed to be read like a map, nor are the objects hooked to the same scale (as they would be in a pictorial rug). Instead, this rug acts a bit like the series of memory-jogging words you might write on cards if you were giving a talk; a quick glance and you are reminded of another story.

One very welcome inclusion in the field in front of the house is the pigs with their super-curly tails. That is not where the two pigs lived, of course; they had a proper sty in the farmyard. One day, Heather asked Uncle Fred what the pigs were called, and he instantly gave them the names Peter and Keith, in honour of the boys, Heather's brothers. Apparently, the boys were very pleased when they heard about this. Not everyone would have seen the benefit of having a pig named after them, so Peter and Keith must each have a good sense of humor.

The Beattie family used hurricane lamps to light Scarcote.

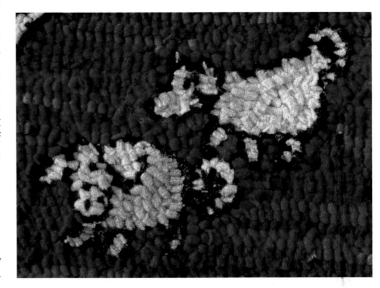

Two pigs with curly tails run free in the field: they actually lived in a sty in the farmyard.

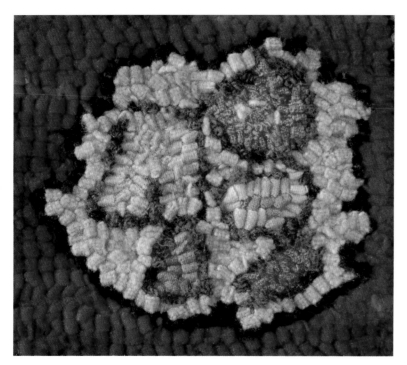

A gorse bush dries a day's washing – a pair of trousers, a skirt and various "smalls".

There is one aspect of this rug that displeased Heather so much that she acted on her threat to "pull it out and re-do it." You would probably never guess that there had been two gorse bushes in the rug until Heather removed one of them, saying that the rug looked "too messy with two gorse bushes near the house." That is one of the joys of rug-making: you can alter the design if it displeases you, even years later (as Heather showed by re-working her grandfather in *Victory Garden,* Chapter 4). If you cannot spot the remaining gorse bush straight away, that is because Old Auntie Beattie has put it to good use, as she always did. How do you put something as prickly as a gorse bush to good use? Old Auntie Beattie dried the washing on it, that is how, and Heather remembers that the dried clothes came in warmed by the sun and smelling of gorse flowers. The clothes and linens were spread across and around the bushes — no pegs needed — and no sensible animal would get close to such a nasty bush just to graze on Uncle Fred's trousers.

On the subject of nasty, there is a spectacularly bad-tempered looking bull in the right-hand gate. One day Auntie Hilda asked Heather, "Where's Mr. Roppo?" Heather takes up the story:

Victor waves his blind person's white cane as the bull snorts behind him.

The Beatties were broad Yorkshire, so 'Robson' came out as 'Ropson' and that got shortened to 'Roppo.' I told Auntie Hilda, 'me dad's gone along the cow pasture.' He'd been visiting the farm since the war when he had his sight. Now he was blind but he still knew every bit of the place very well. He used to tap the stone walls with his stick to find his way around. He knew where the wells, walls, gates, gorse bushes and paths were. He had it all in his head, just like his map of Sunderland. He was quite safe to go off wandering like he did, listening to the birds singing away. But this time Hilda's response was to shout 'oh no, t'bull's in't field!' and she went screaming up the yard yelling 'Mr. Roppo!' and I was hanging off the top of the gate yelling 'dad!' He knew that we wanted him, but he didn't know what we wanted. He could hear our voices, but the wind was carrying our words away. And so there he was, standing right next to the bull and waving his stick in the air and yelling 'yoo hoo' to us… Auntie Hilda was scared stiff because the bull had chased Uncle Reg the day before, and he'd had to jump a wall to get away. Me dad couldn't do that. We were absolutely terrified, but me dad just whistled and shouted and waved his stick as he walked back towards the sound of our voices.

You can almost hear the bull's snorts of disgust as the literally blindly-innocent Victor Robson waves his white stick in its face.

In the field in front of the bull is a tent. Heather's brothers Peter and Keith are approaching it on their hands and knees after a day spent playing in the fields. Heather explains that:

> On one of our holidays there, the boys had a tent and they were camping in the bottom field for a bit of an adventure. While they were out one day, scampering about and exploring the hills, Uncle Fred took a stuffed fox to their tent. The farmhouse was full of stuffed birds and animals, as a lot of houses were in those days, and the fox sat on top of the piano in the parlour. Uncle Fred put the fox in their tent and when they approached it he was hiding around the corner, listening to them screaming. He was always playing practical jokes.

On another occasion, Uncle Fred played a trick that would not work in most modern households. Heather said that, because there was no indoor toilet, everyone had a jerry under the bed to use in the night. "One night, Uncle Fred put a packet of Epsom Salts in me mother's jerry: you can imagine what

A young Heather with an inquisitive, bottle-fed lamb. *Archives of the artist*

Two very different chamber pots posed, purely for effect, by a bed in Heather's home.

Three sheep peer over the dry stone wall which provides a boundary at the foot of this rug.

happened when she got up in the night for a wee! He did some awful things but he was lovely, and all the Beatties were wonderful characters."

There are some sheep peering over the front wall surrounding the farm. "Scarcote was full of sheep but I had nowhere else to put them in the rug," says Heather. "I loved to help with the sheep and lambs whenever I went there."

Heather went to Scarcote more times that she can remember and, once there, she seldom left the farm except to sell butter and eggs in the nearby market or to visit a relative of Old Auntie Beattie's on a neighboring farm. On occasions a little green car took her away from the farm, and it appears top left in this rug. It is a Morris Minor that is being driven by Old Auntie Beattie's great-nephew, Gerald. Heather says:

> I was sweet on him. He was always there and I knew him all my life because he was a few years older than me. He had an old car and, when he visited his aunt and uncle while I was staying at Scarcote, he would take me out in it. During my holidays as a child I'd been no farther west than Hudswell and Scarcote, of course. When I was about 14, Gerald introduced me to places farther up Swaledale like Reeth, Whaw, Arkle Town, Booze and all the other little villages. We went to

Langthwaite where my mother and brothers had lived when they were evacuated during the war. I fell in love with it all.

Without that experience Heather might never have returned to Swaledale, instead writing the whole place off as glorious fun but hard work. As it was, Gerald's guided tours of Swaledale gave her an introduction to the place she has been proud to call home for almost forty years.

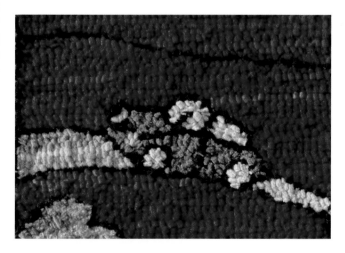

Gerald's car approaches Scarcote to take Heather into Upper Swaledale.

9

Christmas Carols

The original photo Heather took in 1963. *Archives of the artist.*

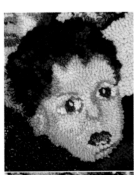

The faces are very detailed and very different.

Heather's working method, with light, medium and dark skin tones, is obvious close up.

The single source for this rug is a photograph Heather took on Christmas Eve, 1963. The children in the photo were in her care for a short time while she worked as a foster mother in a children's home.

This is a picture of my dad playing the piano while the children sing Christmas carols. Those little ones will all be adults now. I wonder where they are and what they are doing?

The colors in the original photo have changed in the years since it was taken. Although Heather took the photo, she cannot remember what the original colors were. She simply replaced the faded colors with brighter ones, using whatever blends she thought would work well together. She used a photograph of the rug as her Christmas card in 2007, printing some of the copies as a sepia version.

When she made *Christmas Carols* the children's faces were the largest that Heather had created in a rug, each of them the size of the palm of an adult's hand. So that she could include every detail of the boys' and girls' faces, she was obliged to make this a large rug. That only increased the joy Heather found in its creation because, to her, the most important aspect of this rug was capturing the children's expressions.

Christmas Carols, fine-cut wool on white linen, 2007. 21 x 22 inches (53 x 55cm). *Collection of the artist.*

Creating faces large enough to have features

These portraits of family member were made in 2008 using fine-cut wool on even-weave Scottish hessian. They show a greater variety of skin tones than Heather has used in *Christmas Carols*. Each rug is about 15 inches (38cm) tall, providing plenty of room to include a lot of detail. Chrissie is at the top in the center, above Vicky, and Laurence is top right. Heather is reluctant to identify the three other faces...

To create faces the size of those in *Christmas Carols*, Heather uses a strict but simple working method. First, she puts in the lightest and darkest areas of each face. "I mark the very darkest areas, the eyes, nose and mouth, first. Then I do the areas which catch the light, the cheeks, chin and forehead, before filling in the areas left empty with mid-tones. The dark shadows and the highlights are vital because they define and hold the space for each face. It's like doing a jigsaw puzzle, mapping out the areas and putting it all together," says Heather.

This technique and the logic behind it are explored in Chapter 12, *The Reeth Parliament*, which tells the story of how Heather first created a large face with hooky.

When depicting a human figure, Heather often uses the jizz — loosely, the essence — of the body's stance as a simple way of making it recognizable. Because they are so close together, these children do not have much body language so Heather needed to make the faces large for the rug to work.

Luckily for me, the boys and girls are all very different; they have fabulous hair and faces. When I started hooking this rug, putting in the light and dark areas, I planned to re-work some of the faces to soften them up. When it was finished I decided I would leave it as it was and I've not pulled one loop out. With all my rugs I tend to go back and pull and tweak and change things but with this one I didn't do any of that. How you see it today is how it was first hooked. I didn't really like all of it but I knew that if I re-worked it I risked losing the essence of the children.

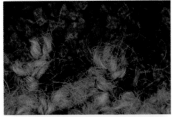

The angles and features of the faces are faithful to the original photo, but Heather has brought her imagination to bear on the hair. She says that hair is always difficult to represent in rugs and claims that she can never get the colors and textures right. In this rug Heather has used a variety of methods to create the different types of hair.

There's Wensleydale sheep fleece, mohair, knitting wool, homespun, regular flannel and tweed. I find hair the most difficult thing about creating people in a rug and I keep a basket of colors just for using as hair. The only tip I can pass on is that it works best if you follow the natural lines of the hair.

The variety of the children's hair in this rug shows that, whether or not it is right in relation to the individual children, Heather can definitely do hair. The rich mixture of colors in the red-headed girl's curls, the delicate loops of fleece in the boy's baby-blond hair and the rich black hair with a patch of light reflected in it show an understanding of the way hair grows and moves. Tweed makes very good hair and the mixed shades it produces look perfect on the child in the mauve jumper.

These eight deliciously different types of hair give each child a unique character.

This jumper is creased around the neckline, giving a clear indication of the position of the body beneath it.

Turning to the children's clothes, Heather says that you must follow the natural lines the garments adopt over the body to give them life and movement. "You don't want any garment to look flat and rigid so you must always bear the underlying body language in mind." As well as being a comfortable and natural fit, the boy's mauve jumper looks really soft and warm with its crew neckline and the girl's pale blue one contains a wide variety of shades. Heather suggests that you should hook the darker lines of the bodies and clothing first, then work on the highlights. After completing the shadows and highlights, fill in the gaps between them.

Victor's jacket is made of an appropriate grey tweed fabric and the directional lines of the hooking define his body very clearly, especially in his arm and the crook of his elbow as he raises his hands to the keyboard. Under his jacket he is wearing a white shirt, a green tie and a brick-red jumper. After losing his sight, learning to make a neat knot in his tie was one of his first priorities. He might not have been able to see it but he wanted to look right for other people. According to Heather, one day he went out wearing shoes which had felt identical to him when he put them on. In fact they were mismatched and one was black and the other was brown. Luckily, he

Below his grey fleck jacket Victor is wearing a brown jumper and a green tie with a white shirt.

was able to laugh at himself when someone told him about his interesting footwear.

Like so many artists working in all sorts of media, Heather finds hands very difficult. The most prominent hands in this rug belong to the pianist. The boy in the white jumper is fiddling with the fingers on both hands, and Heather has captured that gesture and the light falling onto the boy's fingers with her artist's eye; the curve of each finger is lit from the same direction, enhancing their shape and definition.

This child is twiddling his fingers as he sings.

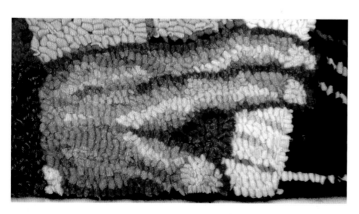

Heather says that she is not happy with this hand, but it mimics the photograph so it must be right.

Heather talked about her father's blindness.

He read these great big Braille books and he'd sit and roar with laughter. He'd get to a sentence with half a word on one line and the other half on the next line and he'd try to fit the two bits together, like "win-" and "dow," but without the hyphens. He said, 'I've got one over on you.' And I asked, 'What's that?' He replied, 'I can read in bed and keep my hands warm under the blankets at the same time!' He had a great sense of humour and he had this huge roaring laugh — it seemed to come up from his toes. He was a fabulous man and his stance was always to have his head tipped slightly back as if he was listening carefully to the world, paying really close attention to the sound of the birds and all the other things he could hear so acutely. That's the essence of my dad — my brothers both recognized him in this rug because after he went blind his head was always up like that. He was a wonderful singer and always sang his heart out. He taught choirs to sing in harmony and he taught my brothers to write music and to create harmonies. I was pleased I managed to capture the essence of him: making this rug was a great joy to me.

The piano Victor is sitting at is almost playable in *Christmas Carols*; the black and white keys are neatly divided and defined and the wood is very richly colored.

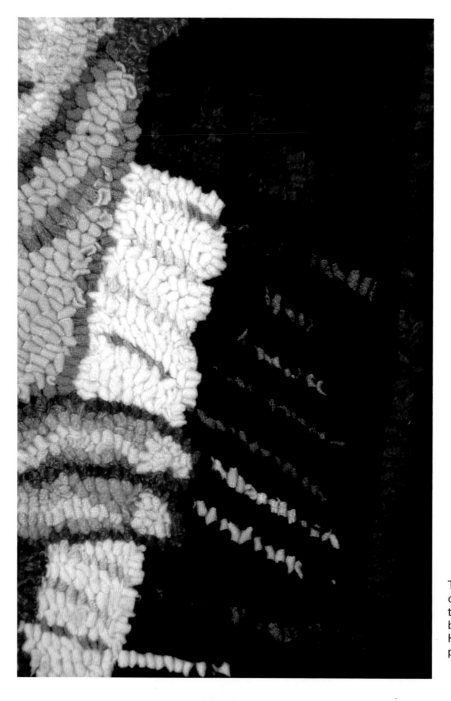

The merest hint of lines of brightness is enough to separate this area of black flannel (a color which Heather rarely uses) into piano keys.

Losing his sight made no difference to Victor's ability as a musician because he had memorised so much of his favorite music and kept it in his head. The youngest of nine children, he was self-taught as a musician and historian because there was no money for extra lessons. Like so many men at that time, his father had no work. Heather said, "I've seen the house they lived in and it's like a little dolls' house. All nine children slept in a little cupboard bed which came down from the wall. One of his sisters used to bake bread and as quick as she was slicing it the others were eating it."

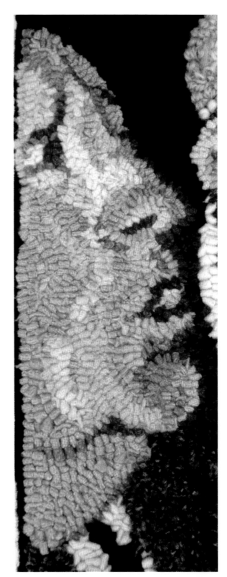

Victor holds his head up in a pose which family members recognise immediately: his eyes are closed and his mouth is open as he leads the singing.

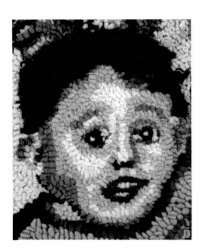

This happy face reflects the enjoyment the children got from singing Christmas carols.

Heather tells another story, based on this rug, about a weekend when she was left in sole charge of the children's home.

I was only 18, not much more than a child myself and the boys and girls knew I was the only person on duty. It was time to make sure they were all in bed, and I was halfway up the stairs when I looked up and saw a sea of children's faces looking down and watching me. I tried to get them to go to bed but they just hooted with laughter when they realized I was trying to be stern. It's not surprising that I had some trouble controlling them after that, and the rest of the weekend was a riot!

The children in Heather's care that weekend would have enjoyed making the most of the short time she was in charge. Heather hopes that they will also have happy memories of spending Christmas Eve 1963 singing around the piano while her father played carol tunes from memory.

This child can only just see over the top of the piano.

10

The Steps

This chapter is devoted to a series of rugs rather than one rug, and these are the only rugs in this book that lie on the floor. They cover the stair treads in Heather's beautiful North Yorkshire home. She rationalizes the damage which the rugs will inevitably suffer as a result of people walking up and down the stairs very simply: "I can always make more rugs to cover the treads." However, she has made sure that potential damage is minimized by using pure wool fabrics for the pile.

Maintenance

A floor rug will need to be beaten free from dust and grit on a regular basis to prevent wear. Heather uses both cylinder and upright vacuum cleaners on her floor rugs. She is not as careful as you might imagine when she uses the cleaner, because she knows that the top-quality backing she uses reduces the likelihood of pulling out any of the loops. If you are not quite as prolific in your rug-making as Heather (who is always looking for a reason to make a new rug), it is probably safer to use a nozzle on the hose of a vacuum cleaner — you can get down deep into the pile this way.

However, as is so often the case with a traditional craft, the time-honoured method of cleaning is the best. Rug-makers of old would hang a rug on the washing line on a dry day and beat it with a flat carpet beater to dislodge the dirt and dust that was trapped in the pile. Beating a rug was also known to keep the moths at bay because, according to an expert Heather consulted, they cannot tolerate such dramatic movement and disturbance of their chosen habitat.

Snow may sound like an unlikely ally in cleaning rugs, but Heather vividly remembers it being used as a form of dry cleaning. During snow storms in the dale, she has seen lines of rugs hanging over dry stone walls. She also recalls seeing rugs laying face down in the snow, being dragged through it, before the dirt was shaken off with the flakes of snow. Heather insists that the snow does not dampen the rugs, calling it a "dry form of wet." She recreated the scene in January 2010 using her rug *The Meadow* (opposite). "The snow isn't like rain, it doesn't soak them," she says. In a similar vein, she can also recall using wet sand to clean the floor at the end of the day when she worked in a shop, and watching her aunt Jessie using spent tea leaves to clean the carpet at home.

Beating is good for rugs, and can be done as often as needed. If you have the space (and your line is strong enough), hang the rug by its long edge and make sure that it is secure — you do not want it falling off and picking up more dirt from the ground. Start beating on the reverse and beat quite firmly across the full width of the top of the rug before moving your beater a little lower down and working back across the rug. Being methodical may sound a bit obsessive, but it will loosen deeply-embedded particles and ensure that they drop down to be beaten free when you work across the lower levels. When the reverse has been thoroughly beaten, beat the front more gently to shake those loosened particles free. If you follow the same top to bottom routine, as many as possible of the loosened particles will eventually drop out of the pile.

There are many old stories about different methods used to clean rugs and Heather tells a lovely one about Mrs. Porter, the wife of the farmer with the stick in *The Reeth Parliament* (see Chapter 12). In their farmhouse kitchen there was a huge rug, far too big for her to move on her own. Naturally, as the kitchen was the hub of the home, the rug got dirty. Every summer, on a sunny and dry day when the farm labourers had a bit of spare time, she would

This rug, *The Meadow*, is lying in snow to be cleaned. Mixed cuts of wool, hooked and prodded on white linen, 2009. 45 x 31 inches (114 x 78cm). *Collection of the artist.*

get the men to drag the rug to the nearby stream where it lay with the clear water running over it during the morning, weighted down with stones to stop it being washed downstream. Just before they came to the kitchen for a bit of lunch, the men would drag the immensely heavy rug out of the water and leave it to dry in the afternoon sun. At the end of the working day they would pick it up and carry it back to the kitchen ready to face another twelve months of muddy boots, animals' feet, cooking spills and so on.

As a general rule, Heather advises against allowing hessian to get wet, but Mrs. Porter's kitchen rug obviously survived the experience. Heather normally uses linen as the backing for floor rugs destined for use at the back door, by the kitchen sink or in children's rooms because she knows they will eventually need washing. Linen backing becomes soft and flexible after washing but, unlike hessian, it is made to be washed so its structural integrity is not damaged by the process.

Heather describes how she cleans her proddy mats with a bucket of soapy water. Laying the mats on a clean-swept paved area in the garden, she pours the warm water over them and uses a broom to work the water into the pile before hanging them on the line to dry in the sun.

The loops in all these rugs are evenly short and the low pile reduces the likelihood of loops being caught and pulled. All of the edges are whip-stitched with the same deep red woollen yarn. In addition to being stuck down with double-sided, heavy-duty adhesive tape, each rug is held in place with dome-headed nails around the three exposed edges. Individual rugs are a very practical way to dress a staircase: if one rug is damaged only that one needs to be replaced, reducing the cost and effort involved in the repair. In addition, they can be taken up and washed if the need arises. These rugs have a hessian backing but Heather knows that she will have to replace them one day, perhaps when she re-decorates the hall and stairs, and is not concerned about weakening the backing.

Despite the fact that all of these rugs were washed before these photos were taken, because they have been in daily use in a busy house for several years, Heather is a little dubious about the merits of showing them in any detail. As a result, there are only whole rug photos except for the two larger rugs.

The first rug you stand on as you climb the stairs celebrates Heather and Les's wedding. It was deepest winter when they were married in Sunderland in January, 1968. Heather has chosen to show the outside of the church surrounded by skeleton trees and snow. Under a watery sky, the stained glass windows are brightly lit from within as the happy couple take their vows in front of friends and family.

The stained glass windows of the church provide a beautiful contrast to the bare trees, grey stone and snow. All rugs in this chapter are 23 x 10 inches (58 x 25cm) unless otherwise mentioned, fine-cut wool on even-weave Scottish hessian.

Les and Heather Ritchie's wedding day, 27th January 1968. *Archives of the artist.*

The rug on the second step (and some others) are friendship rugs that were made by Heather's friends. Because they were not made by Heather, neither photographs nor descriptions of them are included here.

The rug on the third step shows the eldest of Heather and Les's children, Victoria, who was named after Heather's father, Victor. Known to everyone as Vicky, she was born when her parents were still living in the first house they owned, the Grangetown bungalow which had been Heather's childhood home.

Vicky is driving her van, with a fictitious personalized number plate, along a winding moorland road. The road is bordered on each side with the low

The first child born to Heather and Les, Vicky is now a mother herself.

concrete-pillared fences typical of isolated roads in northern England. Sitting alongside the red-haired Vicky is her dog, Lemmy, who went everywhere with her.

The rug on the fourth step represents Les's life at sea, and he has approved this ship and all its details. Heather has used a version of the technique known to film-makers as "day for night" in this rug. By the simple deceit of showing the ship by daylight against a night sky with a crescent moon hanging in the top left corner, Heather has made the ship really stand out from its background.

The ship is one of the Irish Sea ferries Les worked on at the end of his career on the waves. It is tied up in the harbor while a small red van and a larger blue lorry drive up the ramp to reach the lower decks through the stern doors. All the portholes are brightly lit as the vehicles' drivers settle down for a short sleep. The ship's engines send a curling plume of smoke up into the dark blue sky, which means that Les is hard at work somewhere in the vessel's bowels.

Les was a Merchant Navy engineer for much of his working life and sailed all around the world. Heather and the children traveled with him to many destinations and had some terrific adventures, including undergoing the ritual known as "meeting Neptune" when they crossed the equator for the first time. This involves a member of the ship's crew dressing up as Neptune and awarding the "crosser" a certificate after they have undergone a ritual which is normally wet and/or messy.

A red van drives up the loading deck at the back of the ferry whose engines are running smoothly under Les's guidance.

The last step before the two half-landings shows Heather and Les's middle child, their son Laurence.

The vividly-colored background is made of kilts that were woven in a striking combination of red and blue. Laurence, who has inherited his maternal grandfather's musical gifts, is shown playing the piano and appears to be singing. He is surrounded by musical notes.

Greencroft's staircase has two half-landings. Heather has taken good advantage of the opportunity these almost-square treads present to make rugs that show two important aspects of the family's life in Reeth.

The first of these larger steps shows the butcher's shop that gave Les his first break from a life at sea. When the family was living in Rockmount, their first

Laurence has inherited his grandfather's musical ability.

Overton House, which Les ran as a butcher's shop. 23 x 19 inches (58 x 48cm).

home in Reeth, he trained in butchery at Sunderland College. Once qualified he bought the shop, which was known as Overton House, in High Row.

This lovely three-story building has been put to many different uses over the years. Recently it was a cafe offering a take-away service for walkers and cyclists and then, after a major refurbishment, it became a very well-regarded licensed restaurant.

The building was probably erected in the early 18th century and is Grade II listed. There is a substantial house above and behind the shop that Heather, Les and their children moved into when his butcher's shop opened. At that time, the house was very deep and extended a long way back from its stone front. Its depth has since been reduced through the conversion of part of the rear of the building into a holiday home.

When the family moved to Overton House, the children were all young and they enjoyed exploring its many secrets. Chrissie discovered a staircase, hidden in the wall of her bedroom, that led to the room above. The building contained what estate agents refer to as "a wealth of original features" and Heather vividly remembers a set of spice drawers that occupied one whole wall of the kitchen. She was very disappointed when Les gave them away during the refitting work that was essential before he could use the kitchen to process meat products for sale in the shop.

Heather has chosen to show Les opening the shop first thing in the morning. A queue of customers clutching shopping bags is already waiting on the cobbles, and another customer is just emerging from the arched alley alongside the shop. Presumably, he has used this shortcut to reach High Row from one of the many houses to the west of the green.

As Les steps through the open door to greet his customers, we see that he is wearing a traditional red and white striped butcher's apron and has covered his hair. The first person in the queue is a man wearing a dark suit. He has his left hand tucked into his trouser pocket and is holding a red bag in his right hand. The young woman second in the queue is very smartly dressed in a short blue coat with a matching hat. She may be new to the business of shopping for a household, as she does not appear to have brought a shopping bag with her. The older woman alongside her is very warmly dressed with a long coat and a hat and a scarf as well as sturdy footwear. She is probably visiting other shops after the butcher's, as she is carrying a capacious shopping bag. The last shopper to arrive is wearing a traditional flat Yorkshire hat and may have a shopping bag in the pocket of his warm brown coat.

The majority of this rug shows the stone from which Overton House is built. This limestone was probably obtained from one of the area's many quarries. Heather's artistic eye has, of course, brought a broad palette of colors into play in these straight lines of stone. The four almost identical windows are cleverly shown with diagonal lines representing the reflective glass and simple white vertical and horizontal lines for the glazing bars. Heather has added two dark lines for what is virtually the only decorative feature of the outside of the building, the narrow V-shape cut into the stone lintel above the window.

When Les came to sell Overton House, it was bought as a going concern. However, things changed dramatically in the butchery trade in the next few years. The first change was that supermarket chains began to exert pressure on specialist local shops, pressure from which many communities like Reeth have never recovered. Secondly, people started to reduce the amount of meat they ate, for reasons both of health and economics. The butcher's shop eventually closed, and there is no longer a specialist meat shop in Swaledale, except in Richmond.

The first floor window with its stone surround in a wall that has since been painted white.

The queue outside the shop as Les opens in the early morning.

The three Ritchie children look longingly through the window of the baker's shop Les ran. 23 x 15 inches (58 x 38cm).

In contrast, the second half-landing shows Les's other business venture, the baker's shop in Silver Street, Reeth, which is still thriving many years after he sold it. This shop is, literally, just around the corner from High Row where Overton House looks east across the village green. For a while Les ran both the baker's and the butcher's shops at the same time. This was especially exhausting because, after taking on the baker's shop, the family had moved to Hurst. It may be less than five miles (8km) by road between Hurst and Reeth, but Les had to start work at 3am to get bread ready for opening the shop at 8am.

The Ritchies' three children, from left to right and in age order, Vicky, Laurence and Chrissie, peer through the window at the delights their father has been hard at work baking since very early that morning. It must be winter because they are well wrapped up against the dales' biting cold wind. Vicky's red scarf and green coat complement her red hair, Laurence is wearing a dark balaclava helmet and a warm coat, and young Chrissie's blonde curls peep out from under her blue hat and scarf.

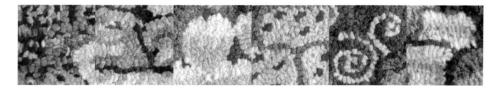

Some very tempting cakes...

The cakes in the baker's shop window are beautifully created in hooky, starting with a rich fruit cake stuffed with bright red glacé cherries and juicy sultanas. Next is a blue-patterned plate piled high with scones, fresh from the oven and already oozing with cream and delicious strawberry jam. There are iced buns, each of them topped with a cherry, slices of a light fruit cake whose cherries have, very obediently, remained evenly distributed throughout the mixture and not sunk to a layer at the bottom, and a luscious chocolate Swiss roll with a creamy filling. Multicolored angel cake is the final sweet temptation before we reach the baker's staple, beautiful cottage loaves with crusty tops.

Behind the children, visible through the glass between the squares of the green wooden window frame, the road climbs away west up the dale. This is a bit of artistic licence, for the shop is not oriented that way to the road, but it reminds us that Les's was the only baker's shop in this part of the dale at one time. The road's steep ascent out of Reeth, up past the school, is captured in a few curving lines of grey wool.

Hall Farm, Hurst, is a very solid building in a peaceful setting.

This is Hall Farm, the Ritchies' family home in Hurst, which they bought during the time Les was running the baker's shop in Silver Street, Reeth. It is a long, low, stone-built dales farmhouse that originally had a cart entrance running right through the building. Heather incorporated the space, which was on the left-hand end of the house, into the living accommodation by putting in an arch-topped window. She has used some artistic licence in giving the hills behind quite such a magnificent height, but there are hills behind the house and they are heather-covered. She modestly describes this rug as "using up scraps from other projects." What marvellous projects those must have been if this is what was left over.

The studio in the garden of Greencroft, Heather's home in Reeth, in mid-summer.

On the next step is a rug that shows Heather's studio in the garden of Greencroft. Since she created this representation of her favorite workplace, the outside has become a lot more disguised by climbing plants. The rowan tree almost in the center is still there, laden with scarlet berries to feed the birds in the autumn. Entering through the door on the left brings you to the office area, and you turn 90° right to go into the studio itself. Since the rug was created, roof windows have been installed in the studio to allow extra light to flood in. Even with the blinds drawn to protect Heather's rugs from fading, these make a huge difference to the amount of light entering the studio.

The flower beds outside the studio are full of color all year round. At the time of year shown in this rug, the height of summer, there are red crocosmia and pink mallow by the water butt outside the door and mauve campanulas under the windows on the right. A purple wisteria hangs over the office window and an apple tree stands in the flower-filled bed to the left of the flagged path in front of the window.

Calver Hill viewed from the east with the Arkle Beck in the foreground, February 2010.

If you turn to the left at the top of the stairs, there are two more steps to climb before you enter the front bedroom.

The first of these rugs is almost photographic in its portrayal of the Ritchies' two dogs, Fleet on the left and Bonnie on the right, and the family's hens and ducks. These animals form a rather unlikely hill-top group standing in front of the rounded summit of Calver Hill, the steep hill to the north of Swaledale and west of Reeth. The landscape in this picture is created with tweedy fabrics and the grey represents the appearance of the lead mining area perfectly.

Chickens, dogs and ducks meet at the top of Calver Hill overlooking Reeth.

Timmy (left) and Zack (right) enjoy the warmth of the Aga which has its shiny stainless steel hotplate covers in place.

The rug on the final step is a lovely scene of domestic tranquillity. On either side of the bright red, oil-fired Aga in Greencroft's kitchen are the two cats that formed part of the Ritchie household at the time Heather created the rug. Timmy, the cat on the left, was a large and friendly tabby, and Zack, on the right, had classic "tuxedo" black and white markings. This scene has changed in that the wall, which was painted terracotta behind the Aga, is now tiled in a profusion of fabulous colors.

Out of sight on the floor in front of the Aga is a traditional, random-patterned, proddy rug on which the current cat, Gizmo, loves to lie. It is wonderful to stand on that rug and lean against the polished, steel, towel rail that runs along the front of the Aga warming yourself on a cold winter's day.

Many of the stories outlined in this chapter will be explored in the rest of this book. The first of these tales, in Chapter 11, uses a rug with a view of Reeth village green to tell the story of how Heather came to be a rug-maker.

Repairs

One of the most satisfying aspects of rug-making is how easy it is to unhook and re-work areas. This is helpful during the creative process, but it is also a useful way to repair a rug. If a rug used on the floor develops a hole, it is usually not only possible to repair it but also quick and easy to do so. Just pull out a few loops in the area surrounding the damage and put in a patch of the same type of backing fabric. Re-work the design using the strips you have removed if at all possible, and hold the two layers of backing together with new loops where the layers overlap.

Heather has never had to repair a linen-backed rug. She loves working with linen fabric for its softness and great strength. In addition, you can wash a linen-backed rug, either in a washing machine (as Heather prefers) or carefully by hand. You should avoid using a hessian-backed rug in a damp environment, because the threads of hessian are weakened by regular exposure to moisture and, more importantly, the backing might shrink. There is more about selecting your backing fabric in Chapter 7, *Guiding Light*.

11

Reeth Village Green

Heather made this rug to celebrate life in Reeth. She has lived in or very near to this small North Yorkshire market town since 1971, longer than she has lived anywhere else. The rug shows her interpretation of the view across the village green from a point somewhere near the Burgoyne Hotel at the green's northern end. Because re-telling the story of creating this rug stirred so many memories in Heather, it is told almost entirely in her own words.

Heather says:

This rug portrays Reeth village green and the higgledy-piggledy buildings surrounding it. I have included my friends because bringing in people you know personalizes your work and gives it a real human interest. There's my much-missed friend, the late Greta Riddell, in her red jacket, walking her dog across the green. My neighbor Evi Squires is coming out of the Chapel with two of her friends. One of the two men I know called John Raw is driving up the road across the green

Reeth from Fremington Edge, with the Arkle Beck in the foreground and the River Swale beyond the settlement.

Reeth Village Green, fine-cut wool on white linen, 1998. 38 x 23 inches (96 x 58cm). *Collection of the artist*

Greta, with a stick to support her, walks her dog on the green.

Heather's neighbor Evi walks across the green with two friends after attending a service in the chapel.

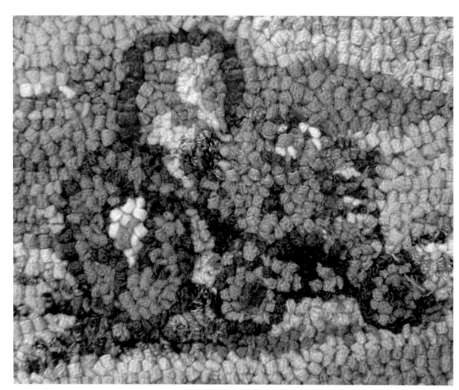

John Raw drives through Reeth on his blue tractor.

in his blue Ford tractor and the other John Raw is herding a few sheep with his dog. I'm sitting on the bench hooking a rug and some visitors to Reeth are sitting on the other bench, enjoying the view. It's a beautiful sunny day in late August, my favorite time of year. That's when the hills are purple with heather and the grass is vivid green, and setting the rug at that time gave me the opportunity to dye a lot of fabric to get the colors I needed.

The buildings around the village green are depicted accurately in this rug—it is definitely a picture of Reeth.

Another John Raw calls to his dog on the green.

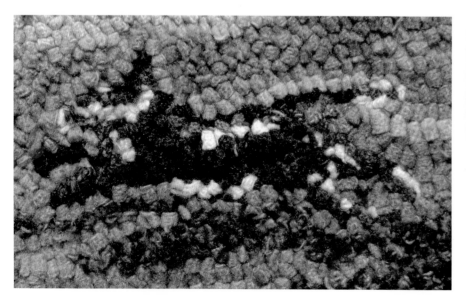

John Raw's dog runs across the green.

Reeth green on a sunny summer's day.

Heather spent many holidays at Scarcote in the heather-covered hills of Swaledale east of Reeth before becoming a social worker in Sunderland. She bought a car as soon as she passed her driving test and immediately offered to drive her parents to Swaledale and to Langthwaite in Arkengarthdale. At first Heather's mother refused to get in the car, saying that she would only go out with Heather at the wheel when she had been driving for a long time! Eventually Eleanor May agreed to risk the journey and they traveled in perfect safety to the dale, where she had a lovely time and met up with friends she had not seen for years.

My dad was blind and I was really worried about him living in Sunderland. He'd had so many accidents, walking into things because the road layouts and the street furniture, lamp posts, bollards, signs and so on, kept on changing and I couldn't be around all the time to be his guide dog any more. When I brought them to the dale we went up to the church of St. Mary in Langthwaite and dad said 'take me to the organ.' He'd played the organ in St. Mary's when he visited my mother and brothers while they were evacuated in Langthwaite. I led him to the keyboard and he sat down, felt for the keys and pedals, pulled out the stops and played as though he'd never been away. I don't think St. Mary's had heard music like that for quite a while. He used to write church music, he was a wonderful composer, a great church man and a member of Christ Church, Sunderland. He was a self-taught musician who earned the respect of the professors at the college my brother Keith attended, the Royal College of Music in London.

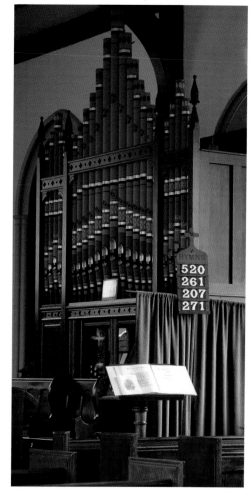

The organ in St. Mary's church, Arkengarthdale, which cost £250 (US$160) when it was installed in 1892.

The heather-covered hills above Reeth.

In this rug there are some sheep grazing on the distant hills, just below the heathery topping near the horizon. It is all in the jizz of course, and each of the sheep is no more than a few loops of white yarn on a purple-grey tweedy background, but there can be no question about their identity: with that jizz, what else could they be?

The sheep on the village green are much more carefully defined, and the essentials of sheep body language are all there. Heads down, grazing on the lush green grass, these clean white fluffy blobs with starkly contrasting black heads and legs and distinctive curly horns are obviously Swaledale sheep.

The ewe that is lying down has her feet tucked underneath her body as she gazes around while resting and ruminating. In truth there are very rarely sheep on Reeth green because the road from Richmond to Muker and beyond crosses it but, as so much of Heather's work demonstrates, a rug can show anything you want it to show.

Sheep on the hills to the south of Reeth.

Sheep grazing on Reeth green.

Lionel, who lives in Fremington about a mile from Reeth. He is very beautiful and friendly, despite not being a Swaledale sheep but rather a Mule/Leicester cross.

The signpost says Reeth and Muker: the name which should be on the left/eastern arm, Richmond, was too long for the available space!

burning in the hearth, the kitchen table was laid with tea ready to be served, and the beds were made and aired with crisp cotton sheets and soft feather pillows waiting for their tired heads.

I bought their old house, the bungalow in Grangetown, Sunderland where I grew up, when they moved to Langthwaite. My mother had said 'we bought this house new when we were first married and I don't want to leave it.' I told her: 'I'm getting married soon and we'll buy it off you.' After getting married in 1968, I lived there with my new husband, Les, until we moved to Reeth in 1971. Our eldest daughter Vicky was born in Sunderland but she didn't walk until we got to Reeth. She first walked in Agnes and Wesley Harker's house at the top of the green.

Because Les was in the Merchant Navy, it didn't really matter to him where we lived. He'd never been to Swaledale and, when I brought him up to the dale for the first time, he immediately fell in love with it. Our younger daughter, Chrissie, and our son, Laurence, were both born in the dale. I'm certain that all three children had wonderful childhoods — they just ran wild with total freedom like I had done on my holidays.

From the moment I moved to the dale I loved it. I love the slow pace: there's no point rushing around because there's nothing to rush for. When you're not racing to catch buses and so on you naturally slow down. It's wonderful.

My new neighbor, Hannah Place, came in and helped me scrub the floors of Rockmount, the first house we bought in Reeth. Hannah said 'you'll want some mats in here for the draughts.' There were no fitted carpets in those days so she came round with her handmade hook, a hessian sack and a bag of old Lisle stockings. I'd never made a rag rug before meeting Hannah and she showed me what to do. My two spaniel puppies, Lady and Blossom, thought it was great fun to eat rugs and they chewed up my first ones!

When I brought my parents up to Langthwaite for a visit they had a lovely time and I got the idea of moving them into the dale. Everybody thought I was absolutely crazy but Jake Stubbs' barn was for sale and I decided they should live there. Against the rest of the family's wishes, I helped my mum and dad move to Arkengarthdale. I called their new home Cherry Tree Cottage because I've always loved cherry trees and have planted one everywhere I've lived, so I did the same for them. On the day my parents moved in, everything was ready for them — there was a welcoming fire

Just like the grass on the green, the grass in the rug is various shades of green from almost blue to nearly yellow.

Two visitors, possibly an older woman and one of her grandchildren, sit on a bench at the top of the green to admire the view.

Because the tradition of rag rug-making is found throughout Britain, there is a rich variety of regional names for the process of making them. The best-known of these include (in alphabetical order) bit, bodgy, broddy, clippy, clooty (from the Scots dialect word for cloth), hooky, list (from the Lancashire word for selvedge), peg (because people used one leg of a dolly peg as a prodder), piece, proddy, proggy, rag, stobby and tabby (from "tabs", bits of waste fabric) and there are many more.

To Heather, the words for the end product are interchangeable and, to her at least, a mat is exactly the same as a rug whether it hangs on the wall or lies on the floor. Whether they are wall hangings or for walking on, the mats and rugs Heather makes receive the same amount of loving care and attention to detail.

Heather has included herself in this rug: she is making a rug whilst sitting on one of the benches at the top of the green.

These houses are recognizable around the green.

Hannah and I made some proddy mats in boring colors. I didn't like them much — they were just utilitarian floor coverings really. But then a lady called Joan Bell moved in next door. She had lived in America for twenty years and rug-making was, and still is, huge and special in America. There are rug schools all across the USA and Joan had been taught by the 'queen of rug-making', Joan Moshimer, who founded Rug Hooking Magazine and also started a company called Cushing Dyes.

Joan Bell showed me the colorful, beautiful, artistic rugs she had made and I thought they were wonderful. She taught me how to dye fabrics, although we had to send to America for the special dyes she used. She showed me how to work with a fine hook, which also came from the USA because stuff like that wasn't available in this country. Rug-making had been huge here before WWII but afterwards, when everyone went over to fitted carpets, there were no more patterns and hooks available. I bought hooks and dyes from America and my rug-making career started. It was Joan Bell who got me going and I've never looked back.

At that point, I went to art classes and did two years of a degree course. Lots of my paintings hang in the house although they're not very good but the course was fun and I learned a lot. I use the theoretical stuff I learned about painting in my rugs because when you work with wools you're painting with fabric.

It doesn't matter how simple a design is — even a child's stick man can be lovely in a rug. I tell my students 'there's no such thing as right or wrong' and I say to them 'don't tell me you can't draw.' The concepts of 'can't' or 'wrong' simply don't exist for me in rug-making. Once you've learned the basic technique of pulling up that little loop you're away. Your design skills will improve over time as you develop an eye for it, when you learn how to really see something, and you'll start to look at things differently.

I filled the house with rugs while I was working as an occupational therapist. I used rug-making in my job for ten years but the bosses were keen to stamp out craft activities, things like basket weaving. The patients loved rug-making but the higher-ups wanted them to do quizzes and things to get their brains going.

Compare this photograph with Heather's version of the buildings (below).

I can't bear a day to pass when I haven't created something. Creating things has been the joy of my life since I was a child when I made dolls clothes. I did City and Guilds courses in Dressmaking and Soft Furnishings years ago. I used to do loads of dressmaking because my hands were always itching to make something.

I dyed nearly all the colors for this rug and there's a lot of over-dyed tweed for the hills. The village green was lovely to do. When the sun shines on the grass it's as bright as an emerald. In an embroidery class someone once said to me 'you can't put these colors together — they don't go' and I said 'God put them together and got away with it, and so can I.' I'm not normally bright but that quick answer just popped out!

These are two buildings at the bottom of the green.

Dyeing – casserole and spot

Swaledale fleece spot and/or casserole dyed with acid dyes.

The processes of dyeing and dip dyeing were explained in *Percival's Bus* (Chapter 6). Casserole and spot dyeing follow the same basic principles, especially with regard to the health and safety precautions you must take when working with acid dyes.

As well as plain flannel, Heather often over-dyes tweeds which contain a selection of colors in their weave. The techniques of dip, spot and casserole dyeing can all be applied to patterned fabric just as easily as to plain but remember that the composition of the fabric will affect the outcome as mixed fibers will behave differently to all-wool fabrics.

Spot dyeing

Heather describes spot dyeing as "like being at play school," and it is a lot of fun as well as very creative. Take your piece of fabric out of the water/vinegar/detergent cocktail in which it has soaked overnight and lay it flat on a white plastic-covered surface. Select your premixed dye liquid and open the jar. Using a spoon kept solely for the purpose, take out a little of the liquid and pour it onto the fabric before spreading and smearing it around, like finger painting. You should be wearing rubber gloves, of course, so you can actually use your fingers if you like. Add a second and third color, if your scheme demands it. When you are happy with the appearance of the piece of fabric, it is time to cook it. If you were to simmer the piece in a pan, as with dip dyeing, the colors would mingle in the water and produce a single (probably very dull) color.

To cook a piece of acid-dyed fabric, you must use moist heat. You can use a microwave, the oven of your kitchen stove or, should you be lucky enough to have one, an Aga. Despite having a beautiful red Aga in her kitchen, Heather prefers to use the microwave in her studio because it is much quicker. She rolls up the piece of fabric, pops it in a plastic bag and places it on a suitable dish with some water in it. She cooks one piece at a time and, in her microwave, a piece will take

seven minutes on full power. After leaving the piece to cool for a few minutes she removes it from the bag, rinses it in a large container of warm water and hangs it up to dry. Heather's washing line on dyeing days is gloriously colorful.

If you use a conventional oven, Aga or otherwise, use a piece of kitchen foil to wrap each piece of dyed fabric separately and leave the parcels in the oven for about an hour. It is important to ensure that the fabric stays damp so the parcels must be tightly wrapped. Heather has no idea how hot the oven is because it is an Aga, but it is always hot. Place an old baking tin in the bottom of the oven with water in it because this is a steaming process which relies on a plentiful supply of water. Whatever happens, do not forget the parcels: Heather once left some in the oven overnight and set the smoke alarm off the next morning when she removed the charred remains!

Casserole dyeing

Casserole dyeing combines dyeing with the cooking needed to fix the color — both processes happen in the same vessel. Place your pre-soaked pieces of fabric or handfuls of fleece (which will end up looking like those in the photo, with luck) in an appropriate-size pan of simmering water, packing them across its width. Wearing gloves, open your containers of dye solution and spoon some of the liquid onto the fabrics, dotting it about at random. Do not put too much fabric in the pan at once or the dye will not reach the lower pieces. Whatever you do, you must avoid stirring the contents of the pan or you will mix up the colors. Leave the pan to simmer for one hour and unpack the magic when it is cool enough to do so safely, rinsing the fabric in warm water before leaving it to dry.

If you need to dye a piece of fabric an even color all over, simply keep the whole piece immersed in the dye bath and move it constantly until it has absorbed as much color as you want. Acid dyes migrate from the water to the fabric and leave the water clear so you can tell when a piece has become as dark as it will get.

Rinsing will indicate whether the dye is fixed and fast. Only a little residue of color should appear in the running water: if dye is pouring out of the fabric into the rinse water, pop it back into the simmering dye pot.

Having laid down all those rules for dyeing you should remember that, in this as in every other aspect of rug-making, Heather loves to break her own rules! She sometimes boils differently colored fabrics together in a pan so that the dyes bleed. This mingling of colors produces some unexpected (and sometimes very desirable) results. It is Heather's old friends, trial and error, again and she suggests that you too can have lots of fun experimenting (safely) with different fabrics and dyes.

To get the buildings right, I took some photos and spot dyed fabrics to produce the lovely colors I needed. The stones have a lot of subtle colors in them, they're not just grey or beige but there's all sorts. I put in a bit of purple and some burgundy, soft green, sandy colors, a bit of gold. After I dyed the fabrics I cut them up and didn't think about how I was using them — I just picked them out of the box at random. If you look at the real buildings closely you can see all sorts of colors in the walls and roofs.

It's all hooked with the same width of strip. I created the outlines first and then put in the windows. I just filled in the spaces between with this random-dyed stuff so the colors made up the stone work for me. I worked in different directions, up and down and round and round, not just in straight rows. If you were doing American clapboard houses you probably should work in straight rows because they are made of wooden planks. Some of my students tend to hook in straight rows and I love to encourage

The chapel is a dominant feature at the bottom of Reeth green.

them to 'break out of the box' and work higgledy-piggledy!

Placing figures in a rug like this can be tricky so I make use of a good tip I got from Anne Winterling, an American rug-hooker. She showed me how she uses cut-out paper figures, playing around with their positions on the backing until she is happy with them. You can cut figures out of magazines or use specially-taken photos if you need something really different. It's a fun way to predict what your rug could look like, and it can save a lot of time re-hooking when things don't work out.

Hooky is my favorite technique because you can be so relaxed as you work. Rug-making is the best form of therapy there could ever be!

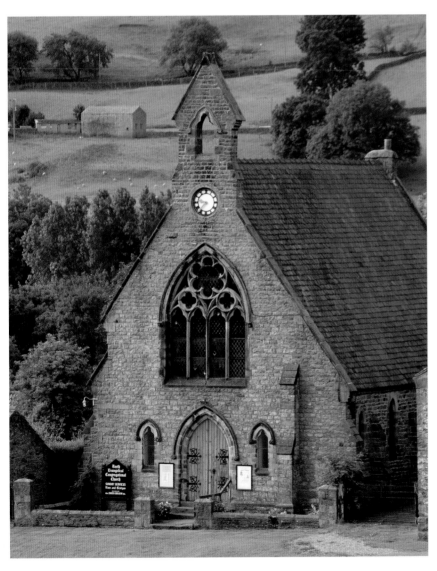

The Congregational chapel in Reeth.

12

The Reeth Parliament

Although this is a memory rug for Heather, its content is also significant to other residents of Reeth as well as to its many visitors. A picture of the rug appears on the information panel adjacent to the shelter at the top of the village green. It was in this shelter that the photograph Heather used as her source was taken. The original photo formed part of an article in *The Northern Echo* and this rug has appeared in that newspaper, as well as on Tyne Tees Television and in several magazines. It is probably the most popular rug Heather has made.

Heather based her design on this lovely photo by Gavin Engelbrecht. *Courtesy of The Northern Echo.*

The Reeth Parliament, fine-cut wool on monk's cloth, 1997. 28 x 15 inches (71 x 38cm). *Collection of the artist.*

Comparing the rug and the photo will show how faithfully Heather has reproduced the figures. She has echoed the excellent balance of the photograph in which the men's hands and feet are arranged symmetrically. Even the colors form a reflected pattern across the stone bench on which the five men are sitting. Heather has omitted some intrusive and unnecessary details, like the notice board top right, and she has enlarged the area of wall around

Victoria. In the 1930s, the parish council added walls and a roof to give local people sitting there some protection from the wind and rain. Evi remembers that the roof was built by Blenkiron's, the local builder, and that it took four men to carry the roof across the top of the green from their workshop.

This was the first rug Heather made that contained faces large enough to have features. The small figures in her earlier rugs had included only a

The reverse (composed from a series of close-ups) shows more clearly how Heather created each figure using directional hooking.

the group to further balance the image. The men (left to right) are Frank Kendall, Alan Sunter, Maurice Porter, Fremmie Hutchinson and Robert Franklin. Fremmie was famous for being the last lead miner in Swaledale, although he also worked as a farmer and had been the landlord of the highest pub in England, Tan Hill at the top of Arkengarthdale. His first name was Fremont which came to him via relatives who had emigrated to America in the 1840s.

The composite view of the back of the rug has been reflected so that it looks like the front. It shows how Heather has followed the dynamic lines of the clothing to produce realistic body shapes. It also shows how closely she has spaced the lines of hooking.

Sadly, all these men are dead now and no-one has replaced them in the shelter. Of course there are still old men around but you don't see them. Perhaps they stay in the pub putting the world to rights instead of sitting in the shelter like these men did.

According to Heather's neighbor and friend, Evi, the shelter started life as a simple wooden bench seat with a bar across the back. This bench was erected in 1887 to celebrate the Golden Jubilee of Queen

few light-colored loops to mark the space where a face should appear. This was not the only way she avoided creating detailed faces, and giving someone a big hat or showing only the back of their head are also useful tricks. Heather's reluctance to tackle faces with features came, quite wrongly, from assuming that what she could not do in painting or drawing she would not be able to do in rugs.

If you are ever in Reeth, do not call this "the bus stop" – it is the shelter where the Reeth Parliament met!

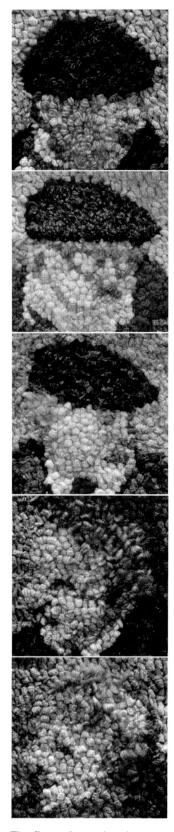

Heather made this rug in America as part of her first figurative class with Roslyn Logsdon. She wanted to make a rug that depicts life in the dales. She chose this image because, as she said, "these five men knew everything that was going on and they would sit in the shelter every day." Heather found the prospect of making a rug based on this photo very exciting but she did not know how she was going to start. When she got to the class, Roslyn told her "just go for it. Put the dark areas in first, then the light areas and just fill in the rest." Roslyn gave this advice despite the fact that, as Heather says, "she often gives her figures blank faces. I like to add features to the large faces I make and it was Roslyn who opened up the world of figurative rug-making for me."

This technique works because it relies upon the fact that you can tell what something is simply by recognizing the pattern created by the lightest and darkest areas. Think about what happens when you see a friend across the street — you do not need to be able to see the color of their eyes to recognise them. The shape of their face is adequately defined by the broad light width of their forehead, the dark shadow beneath their chin, the light and shade of their cheeks and eye sockets.

Heather tells of the moment she realized she had mastered the technique.

> It was very fine work and, naturally, I was very close to it. At that distance, it didn't look like anything at all. But when Roslyn came over and saw it she said 'Heather, that's amazing' and took it to the other side of the room. After resting my eyes for a moment I looked up and, when I first saw it from farther off, the hairs on the back of my neck stood up. Suddenly I could see the faces I'd created, and it was recognizably the group of men I knew as the Reeth Parliament! I'd hooked it using fabric but I couldn't have painted or drawn it. The rug got rave reviews in America and appeared in *Celebrations* magazine.

The five animated and attractive faces.

The reverse of the five faces, showing the light, medium and dark skin tones.

The Reeth Parliament was made in a week using pure wool fabrics. The faces and hands are made of dyed new flannel and Heather used recycled fabrics, including tweeds — "tweeds are lovely to work with" — for the clothing and the wall. She took the tweeds with her to the USA and bought some of the flannel in the rug school.

The five pairs of hands (composed from a series of close-ups) say a lot about the character of each man.

Preparing and cutting pile fabrics

Heather explains her method for preparing fabric for use in a rug.

I wash everything before it comes into my studio. This is especially important with recycled fabrics, both to improve the smell and to wash out any moths. Washing new fabric is important because it removes the dressing and softens the fabric. The mechanical action of washing will also mat the fibers of new fabric a bit, binding them together slightly so the fabric is less likely to fray when you cut it into strips. Everything is washed on a normal warm wash, not boiled.

People often phone Heather to ask for advice on cutting a particular type of fabric and her answer is nearly always the same: "cut it and see—you can't tell otherwise." As was explained in Chapter 5, *The Evacuees,* you must cut all woven fabrics except tweed on the grain—along the warp or the weft— that is, the direction in which you can tear it. Tweed is different because it can shred and drop to bits if cut on the grain. To overcome this, cut it on the cross, the bias, to get a stretchy piece with a wavy edge.

Heather would not normally use woven cottons, especially in floor rugs, because they flatten and get dirty very quickly, but she does use knitted cotton T-shirts that can be cut in any direction. Heather observes that Australian rug-makers use a lot of cotton T-shirts in their work because they do not have access to a good supply of wool sweaters. As a result, Australian rugs are always brightly colored and vibrant. In the Rug Aid workshop in The Gambia (see Chapter 18, *Origins and Identities*), trainees make use of whatever fabrics are available including donated tailor's scraps. There are often T-shirts for sale in the local market, although the stall-holders are always surprised when they find out how Heather plans to use the shirts.

This corner of Heather's garden studio in Reeth houses a chest of drawers stuffed with strips.

Heather says:

I am passionately in love with wool, it's alive for me and I think it is the most wonderful fabric in the world. I can make it do anything and it talks to me, sings to me. I can dye it any color I want — it's just magical. I buy plain white wool flannel from Halifax, West Yorkshire. A friend in Durham went to a mill there and the guy said 'I've made this wool fabric for America but it's got a flaw in it,' so we got it cheap. When he realized we liked it he said he'd make us some. I don't know how often he'll make it for us but it's wonderful stuff. I bought a lot just in case he doesn't make any more! We used to get fents — offcuts, remnants: call them what you like — and I would fill the car with them. I couldn't create some of the effects I can achieve now if I didn't have good white flannel to dye.

Work this detailed is done with the finest strips you can cut without the fabric splitting. Each of these strips is just three or four threads wide. If you're going to cut fabric that fine it must be top quality flannel and it needs to be washed first so the fibers cling together. That very slight felting means you can cut it into fine strips with a machine.

With the faces, I started by putting in the dark areas. Next I put in the highlights where the sunlight is catching them. Finally I filled in the medium tones between them. There's not a lot of detail, really — the faces are actually very simple. If you look closely at them, they look like nothing on earth! When you get a little distance away from the rug the faces appear as if by magic. One of the most important lessons I've ever learned is Paul Valéry's phrase 'to see is to forget the name of the thing one sees.'

This method of working was referred to in *Victory Garden* where Heather aimed to create the general impression of vegetables rather than their detailed construction.

In this rug I had to include feet and hands, things I knew I couldn't draw or paint. I didn't have any idea at all how I was going to represent them using hooky. I just couldn't work it out until I forgot what they actually were and saw them as simple geometric shapes. When they stopped being hands and feet they became positive and negative shapes. When that happened, I forgot what I was

The five pairs of feet (composed from a series of close-ups) complete the hooky description of each man in the Reeth Parliament.

Trace and transfer #1

Left to right: Heather made a black and white photocopy enlargement of the image and used a black pen to go over the most important lines of the picture; she placed a piece of dressmakers' net over the enhanced image and drew those vital lines onto the net; the resulting outline enabled her to re-draw the image, using a black pen whose ink went through the net, onto the backing.

If your source photo is in color, photocopying it in black and white will reduce the multitude of shades of color to their intensities of grey. This will enable you to differentiate the light areas from the dark ones much more easily, and you will use these differences to create the main lines of your design. Do not be afraid to take this opportunity to amend or simplify the source photo, if needed. *Kids in Clover* (see Chapter 13) is a good example of a rug made from an amalgamation of photos and *The Reeth Parliament*, a lively and interesting rug, is a simplified version of the original photo. *The Ha'penny Ferry* (see Chapter 3) is a good example of simplification coupled with imaginative introduction of color, and *Victory Garden* (see Chapter 4) took one small image and made a whole rug around it.

Enlarge your photo or drawing, if needed, and use a soft pencil to trace the main elements onto dressmakers' net. These main elements are the darkest or lightest areas of the picture, such as the deepest shadows, the brightest highlights and the major body movements. Pin the net onto the backing and go over the pencil lines with a black felt-tipped pen. This will transfer the most important lines of the picture onto the backing.

Keep your photocopy and the net you traced over it, at least until you are happy with the way the design appears on the backing. It can be helpful to keep the black and white photocopy until the rug is complete so that you can refer to it if you start to lose your way with the lights and darks.

If you cannot make a black and white photocopy of your source for any reason, you could make your own drawing of the item using a grid to get the proportions correct. You can use net to trace and transfer your drawing in the same way, or you can use a lightbox to trace the light and dark areas. Modern technology means that you can even create designs on a computer and use your printer to make a transfer which will put your original design onto the backing when you iron it. Amazing! What would our grandmothers have made of that?

Above all, remember that the lines you lay down in this trace and transfer process are only a guide for your hooking — you can always remove loops and re-work an area until you are completely happy with it.

Left to right: the lightbox – a pair of bright tubes at the bottom of a sturdy wooden box topped with toughened glass; the photocopy is placed on the glass and the hessian is laid over the top – the photo is dark to show how the light shines through the two layers; with flash illuminating the top, you can see the pins on the back which are holding the two layers together to prevent movement.

working on and just got on with hooking the positives first, filling in with the negatives. If you forget what you are working on you can even work upside down.

As soon as my brain remembers to think of them as feet or hands, I remember that I can't do feet or hands. It's much easier to work if I forget the name of the thing I am seeing. Having said that, you have to remember that all the parts of the body are three-dimensional and you need to hook along the lines which define them. Curved lines are vital when you are making a two-dimensional representation of a three-dimensional shape because flat straight rows can never produce a realistic appearance.

I drew the design on the front of the white linen backing. I always spend some time deciding what size to make a rug. The width of the strip determines how many loops you can get in across the rug, and that governs how much detail you can include. I cut these strips as fine as I could. There wasn't much detail in the faces in the photo

so most of the definition comes through the body language and shapes. I enlarged the photo, and copied it in black and white which made the main dark lines and shadows really stand out.

Heather used the trace and transfer technique to establish the proportions and positions of the figures but she hooked the background freehand.

I kept the palette of colors in the area around the figures pale because the stone wall in the background is an important feature, but I didn't want to lose the figures into it.

I copied the colors of the men's clothing quite accurately but I didn't dye any of the fabrics except the skin tones. There's a blue boiler suit and a red tie, but you can always use artistic licence to change whatever aspects you want to. I didn't re-create the Fair Isle sweater, for instance. I was so pleased with this rug — I couldn't believe that it wasn't a fluke so I created the three children next.

Detail of the wall.

13
Kids in Clover

Heather hooked *Kids in Clover* immediately after finishing *The Reeth Parliament* (see Chapter 12). She was so astonished at her success in creating a likeness in that rug that she felt the need to make another one very quickly to check that it had not been just a fluke. Among other fabrics, she used the leftover scraps of flesh-colored flannel she had bought in the USA for *The Reeth Parliament*. The rug's name was later suggested by her fellow rug-maker Anne Ashworth when Heather offered the rug for an exhibition, apologizing for the fact that it did not have a title and saying that it was just a rug of her "kids."

The rug shows Heather's three adult children, (left to right) Vicky, Laurence and Chrissie, sitting together in the garden of the family home in Reeth, North Yorkshire. From a rug-making point of view, Heather is lucky that her three children have very different hair, personalities and body language.

She has exploited some of these differences very well in this rug, for instance in emphasizing Vicky's vividly-colored locks, Laurence's short dark hair and Chrissie's luxuriant golden curls.

Each of the figures contains an amazing amount of detail, showing just how finely she cut these strips. Vicky, for instance, is holding an open can of beer — you can see the liquid through the ring-pull hole on the top. Around her neck is a leather thong with a floral pendant. Laurence's T-shirt features a large logo, and Chrissie is wearing a sleeveless top and a necklace.

I was thrilled to have captured the kids' likenesses, and this technique is what I'm known for now. People come to my classes and say 'I can't possibly do anything like that' and I tell them 'of course you can: if I can do it, so can you,' and they do!

Vicky.

Laurence.

Kids in Clover, fine-cut wool on white linen, 1997. 19 x 11 inches (48 x 27cm). *Collection of the artist.*

Trace and transfer #2

In *The Ha'penny Ferry* (see Chapter 3), Heather worked from a small photograph so she made a series of photocopies of the image, a section at a time, to enlarge it to the size she needed. After sticking them together to make one picture of the right size, she traced the main lines of the design onto dressmakers' net and put the photocopy to one side. (Heather points out that rug-makers in the USA often use "red dot" tracing fabric for this part of the trace and transfer process.)

She followed a similar routine for *Kids in Clover,* except that her source material was two separate photographs which needed to be enlarged before she added the background by simply looking at her surroundings. Only part of *Kids in Clover* was traced — the rest was drawn straight onto the hessian using the garden as inspiration. Heather drew the first drafts in chalk so she could alter lines easily as she worked.

When the net version of the image was complete, Heather cut a piece of hessian the size of the finished drawing plus the narrow border and a further four-inch (10cm) margin all around for finishing. After pinning the net securely to the hessian, she used a black felt-tip pen to draw along the lines of the design on the net. As she drew, the ink went through the net and transferred the image to the hessian.

This rug uses a lot of fabrics that were dyed especially for the purpose. Some of this is new flannel, like the skin, hair and Vicky's beautiful draped top, and some is over-dyed tweeds, like Chrissie's wonderfully-rich skirt and the Lloyd Loom woven chairs Vicky and Laurence are sitting in. All of the fabric is wool.

Revealingly, Heather's range of colors for skin is very small. "I only use three skin tones, light, medium and dark." Where the difference is as minute as it is between the three shades Heather used in these faces, you only need to vary the quantity of dye you use by a tiny amount. Heather used a toothpick to add a very small amount of dye to a pan for the first batch of fabric, and doubled up the amount for each of the next two batches of fabric to achieve increasing intensities of color. Heather stresses how important it is to use the same quantity (by weight or area) of fabric in each batch.

The reverse of this rug is an interesting lesson in technique. As Heather herself says, "round the back you can clearly see how I built up the images. I'm only aiming for an impression of the thing or person — if I can capture their essence, their soul, that's enough." You can also see where Heather has left small spaces between loops to help the rug breathe, to relieve the tension on the backing fabric.

Chrissie.

Heather's painterly touches are visible on the reverse. For instance, look at the dark line around Chrissie's face, a shadow which serves to define the change from skin to similarly colored hair. The dark area surrounding Chrissie's blonde hair, which keeps the curls distinctly separate from the background, stands out much more clearly here than on the front of the rug where it is hardly visible.

There is another lesson to be learned by looking at the straight lines which form the glazing bars of the studio windows. On the reverse it is easy to see that Heather has hooked them in dead straight lines but they lose some of their definition in the loops on the front, even though these loops are quite low. This is the inevitable result of hanging up a rug made of loops with even a little bit of height. Looking back at *The Steps* (see Chapter 10), the extremely low loops led to very clear definition which is retained despite the friction of feet on the rugs. Part of the reason for this is that those rugs have always been kept horizontal and are subject to equal movement in both directions, up and down. A loop which stands proud of its vertical backing will always flop over downwards a little, particularly in loosely-worked directional hooking.

Chrissie and Vicky, front and reverse of rug.

The reverse of the whole rug.

Heather used green carpet tape to finish off *Kids in Clover*, but she could have used strips of any strong fabric. She proudly points out that she remembered to put a label on this rug. This rug has a backing of white cotton monk's cloth that Heather confesses she does not really like, although she will admit that it is very soft and easy to work on.

The reverse also shows just how much some colors have faded, particularly the blue, purple and red, despite Heather's taking care to keep the rug out of direct sunlight as much as possible. The detail from *Little Bo Peep* shows even more dramatically how some colors, especially blue, are light-fugitive. This is part of a headboard Heather made for Chrissie, her youngest child, in the 1970s. As the reverse was hard up against a wall for most of its life, the colors have stayed out of the sun and remained bright and lively: it must have been a lovely item when new.

Details from *Little Bo Peep* showing dramatic fading.

Vicky and Laurence, original photo. *Archives of the artist*

Chrissie, original photo. *Archives of the artist*

Heather has made some changes between the source photos and the rug that reflect the fact that you can do anything you want when making a rug. She stuck two pictures together to get this image and enlarged the background, so that *Kids in Clover* covers a much larger area than the source photos. Coupled with a few other tweaks, these changes enhance the sense of harmony and balance in the rug.

In front of the figures, joining them together, is an entirely fictitious low hedge. This is not intended to resemble actual plants, just to give an impression of dense hedging. Heather has used a wide variety of different shades of green, some of them over-dyed tweed for an even greater range of color, and some small areas of white for flowers. This was all that she needed to create the feeling, the jizz, of a hedge.

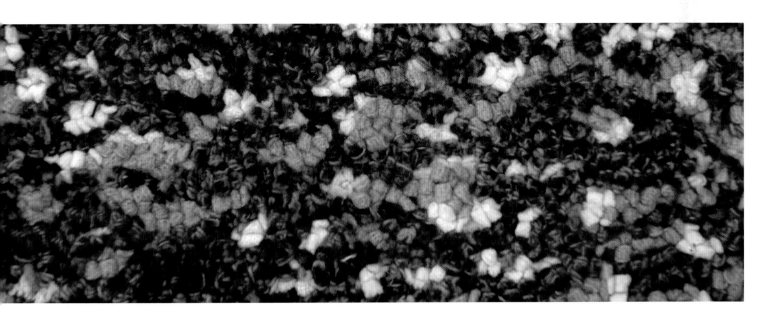

The hedge, which Heather invented to unite the three people and extend the picture.

The background accurately reflects the surroundings of Greencroft, the house Heather has lived in for 15 years. The details of what she sees in and from her garden are contained in this rug, even though this is not precisely the view she enjoys everyday. The hill behind Laurence and Chrissie is Fremington Edge which rises about 820 feet (250m) above and to the north east of Reeth. In this section of the rug, the straight lines of the peaceful sky accentuate the almost random lines of the area below the Edge itself. This is recognizable as the erratic scree slopes and the scattered patches of vegetation growing on them, growth which contains bracken, heather and gorse scrub as well as rough grass.

One of the joys of Heather's life is that she can see Fremington Edge from her garden, studio and home. During the course of a day, this steep limestone slope changes its appearance dramatically. In the early morning, it may be mist-shrouded, hazy and looming. If bright sunshine falls on Fremington Edge during

Fremington Edge from the garden of Greencroft, February 2010.

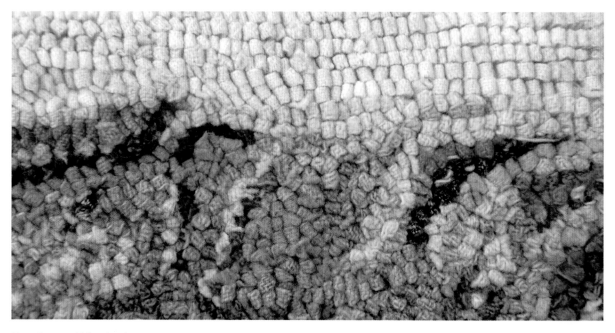

Fremington Edge in the rug.

The studio.

the day it looks inviting, if the day is wet it can look forbidding. Whatever the day's weather has been, it is always at its most beautiful in the evening. Then it is bathed in shades of red and orange as the setting sun, shining along the dale, strikes it.

That part of Greencroft which the outside world sees has changed very little since the Ritchie family moved in, but the garden and the interior have both been transformed into riots of color. The main change indoors has been that the internal walls are now clothed in rugs and paintings, making it a very warm and welcoming home. Like all good gardens, Greencroft's is a bit of a law unto itself and it can be difficult to "keep on top of it" at times (as Heather says she should do), but the variety and quality of the plants in it shows that its creators have a keen appreciation of color and a good understanding of shape and form.

Vicky and Chrissie are both talented rug-makers in their own right. In addition, as a qualified rehabilitation officer for people with visual impairments, Chrissie has taught mobility and other skills to blind and visually impaired students at the GOVI school during several of Heather's visit to the Rug Aid project in The Gambia. (There is much more about this in Chapter 18, *Origins and Identity*.)

The building behind Vicky is an earlier incarnation of the studio Heather uses every day that she is at home, the studio which appears in *The Steps* (see Chapter 10), although it is now almost covered with colorful plants. This is also where Heather dyes fabric and cuts it into strips as well as where she occasionally teaches small groups. Most of her rugs are made indoors, sitting in front of the fire, or in what she calls her fairy grotto in the garden. The studio also houses Heather's massive collection of fabrics and a supply of backing and finishing materials, as well as her many scrapbooks, ideas files and mood boards.

The differences between Heather's many mood boards tell you that her creative process is variable, but for most rugs she gathers together swatches of

This corner of Heather's studio contains baskets of strips and dyed fleece.

color (threads, wools, fabrics and paint samples, for instance) and textures (which might be small pieces of textiles, fleece, plants, or embossed paper) and adds images that inspire her (pictures cut from magazines of faces, landscapes, animals, buildings; photos she has taken without a rug in mind; photos taken whilst a rug was in the planning) as well as writing words on the board (soft, purple, brick, light, moon, grass, hot, daisy — anything that relates to the rug). This is less about design, what goes where, and more about the feel of the rug; a good mood board is an invaluable tool.

Heather sometimes jokes about moving out of Greencroft into a smaller house in Reeth. Deep in her heart she knows that this will not happen for a long time, not least because the "kids" in this picture love their family home almost as much as she loves it.

The shelves in Heather's studio where garments and fabrics are stored before being cut into strips.

Record keeping

Heather's difficulty in remembering some of the details surrounding most of the rugs in this book prompted her to make a very good point about sources and record keeping in rug-making. She suggests that you should use a piece of plain fabric, perhaps a length of carpet tape, as a label on each rug. Using a permanent marker, you should write details like your name, the rug's title and the date you finished it. When all the details are recorded and the ink is dry, sew the label to the back of the rug. Although she advocates recording the details of the creation of every rug, including where your ideas come from, she freely admits that she does not always do so. "One of these days," she says, "I'm going to remember to write on the back of all my rugs," and then she laughs before adding, "now that you can print onto fabric using transfers made on the computer, it should be easier to keep records in future. It's something I've got to get around to doing!"

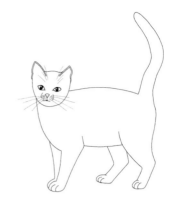

14

My Animals and Other Family Members

Jackdaw Jeans, My Little Bonnie, Fleet, Timmy, Bearing Gifts — and life in Hurst

Jackdaw Jeans

The tiny hamlet of Hurst has previously been mentioned and the rugs in this chapter nearly all relate to the time the Ritchie family lived there.

Hurst was once a much larger community than it is now. It sits high on the virtually tree-less and windswept moor less than two miles (3km) to the north east of Reeth as the crow flies. When lead mining was an important activity in the area, the ore was dug and smelted at Hurst as it was in so many small communities in Swaledale. On census night in 1841, when lead mining had already started to decline in importance, almost 350 people of all ages were living in Hurst in fewer than 60 family groups. About 100 of these people used the word "lead" when describing their occupation. By 1851 only about 40 people earned their living from lead, a figure that fell to around 30 by 1881. By 1901, the population had fallen to around 75 people and nobody earned a living from lead. Many of the houses are now holiday homes and the settlement looks and feels very spread out these days, although Heather is pleased that there are about half a dozen farms in Hurst that are still going strong.

Hurst is first represented by the rug called *Jackdaw Jeans*. This is based on a photograph, taken by Heather's son Laurence, which shows a jackdaw sitting on a pair of his jeans on the washing line in the garden of Hall Farm, Hurst. As was mentioned in *Victory Garden* (Chapter 4), Laurence was a keen ornithologist. The jackdaw which is the subject of this rug was one of the many birds brought to him for rehabilitation after suffering an injury. By the time it was well enough to return to the wild, this jackdaw had become thoroughly domesticated and Laurence adopted it as a pet.

Heather tells the story: "Laurence had a pet jackdaw called Sooty." Heather's Sunderland accent means that she pronounces it "SUE-tea". "Sooty lived in the house and slept in Laurence's bed. I'd put a towel on his pillow, and I have a photo somewhere of the two of them asleep," she said.

The photo that inspired the rug. *Courtesy of Laurence Ritchie*

Despite being one of the smaller elements in the rug's design, the jackdaw is its focus. This is partly because it is the darkest element and, furthermore, a dark element on a light background. The jeans immediately below it are its design opposite, a light element on a dark background and, despite being larger, they are less prominent. The two vertical halves of the rug are beautifully balanced.

Jackdaw Jeans, various cuts of wool on even-weave Scottish hessian, 1985. 30 x 24 inches (76 x 60cm).
Collection of the artist

The jackdaw has his beady eye on the viewer, something that is felt rather than seen until one is very close to the rug. The fabrics used to create his head include a lot of light-catching, sparkling textiles. The feathers on the body of the jackdaw contain a lot of different colors, in exactly the way that the feathers of the living bird are not simply black. Heather has used a little bit of fleece as well to replicate the way the bird's feathers sometimes became ruffled, and has included more of the sparkling fabric on its wings. It could almost be that the bird is wet. She says that she added the fleece long after completing the rug. It is hard to believe, but this was one of Heather's very first hooky creations made long before she did very much dyeing or really fine work.

The jackdaw's legs are just as spindly as those of a living bird. Whatever the species, a bird's legs seldom look strong enough to support the body above them. Heather has copied the downward curve of the jackdaw's tail perfectly.

The bird's feet are not depicted, but they are clearly spaced wide apart. This is how many birds will stand when their footing is not secure, almost like two legs of a tripod. This is a fine-looking bird, obviously in the best of health. No doubt he was well-fed when he lived with Laurence, getting table scraps as well as special bird seed. In the wild, jackdaws eat insects and other invertebrates as well as weed seeds, grain, discarded human food, stranded fish and food from bird tables. Laurence would have done his utmost to provide it with a suitable diet.

The jeans upon which the jackdaw is standing are secured firmly to the line with wooden clothes pegs and the line is held up in the air with a stout wooden prop. Both of these elements of the design are created using hooky and are made of dyed flannel, whereas the white flannel of the washing line is un-dyed. Heather observes that un-dyed flannel is more often cream rather than white. In this rug the color was far from vital, but the *Fleet* rug in this chapter demanded white flannel.

The jackdaw.

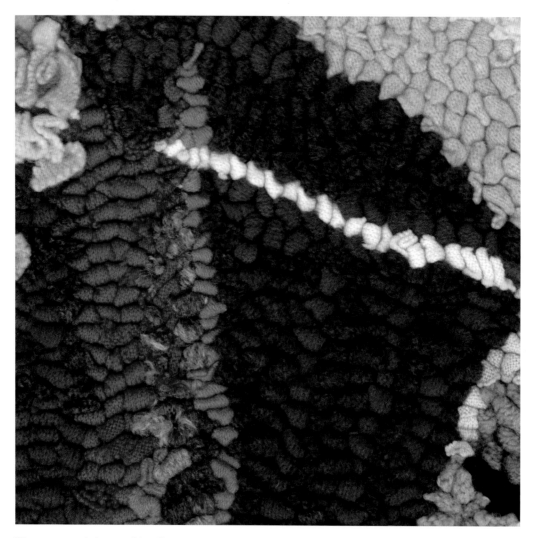

The prop and the washing line.

The prop is another example of Heather's understanding of the technique of representing three-dimensional objects in two dimensions. On the side out of the sun, the wood is dark and plain with no visible details. The other side, which is lit by the same sunlight that is making the jackdaw's feathers sparkle, is richly-detailed and one can almost feel the texture of the wood. The angle of the prop against the dark background is emphasized by the difference between the directions of the lines of hooking Heather has used in these two areas.

The sky is beautiful and understated. Judging by color alone, it is hard to say where the sky stops and the hills start. In fact a band of cream marks the lowest part of the sky and the dark blue area below it is the top of the hills beyond Hurst. The clue to the distinction between the two lies in the direction of the lines of hooky. Heather has used straight lines to make the sky but the lines of the hills below follow the contours of the landscape.

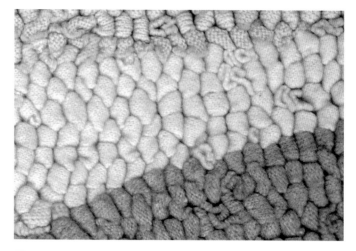

The sky immediately above the hills.

"When you are up above the rest of the world, as you are in Hurst, the sky seems enormous," says Heather. "If you stand on one spot and turn in a circle wherever you look, low down, you see the horizon with the vast sky opening up above it. At night, the sky is jam-packed full of stars because there are no street lights to spoil the complete darkness."

This is a vaguely threatening end-of-the-day sky, and maybe the jackdaw is wet having flown back to the washing line from a rain shower not very far away. The lines of grey with a painterly wash of blue suggest rain-containing clouds while the tiniest trace of pale pink in the lowest fold of the hills suggests that the sun is going down.

"One of the advantages of living above the rest of the world like this is that the sun shines all day or, rather, it's light all day," says Heather. "Unlike houses on the valley sides, there's not a time of day when the sun is hidden from view behind the hills opposite." For an artist this has one important result. Between sunrise and sunset there is no time of day when it will become hard to work because the light fades.

The trees on the left-hand side of this rug are intricate and fascinating. The majority of the tree area is made from sweaters which Heather happened to have available and they were used "as is". Like the rest of the rug, the trees are made using hooky but they look like dense proddy in places. This is another example of Heather's use of cut high loops. This time, the tops of the loops have been sheared off leaving the free ends only a little bit higher than the intact hooky loops around them. Heather wanted to retain the density and to avoid the floppiness which results from leaving long loose ends.

To make a real feature of this way of working, Heather used slightly wider strips to make these loops for the trees. She also used a slightly under-sized hook to pull them through the backing. In combination, these two features led to the fabric strip becoming doubled-over. After cutting the top off the loops Heather ended up with tightly-curled and densely-packed fabric which looks like impossibly closely-worked proddy. The curl is irregular, which enhances the resemblance to something organic. To further enhance the effect, "I used sweaters which naturally curl when cut into strips," says Heather.

Because they stand slightly proud of the background, you can see the texture of these cut loops really clearly among the hooky work. This technique could be used to good effect in a wide range of subjects, from tight curls in a child's hair to the ripples in sand on the beach.

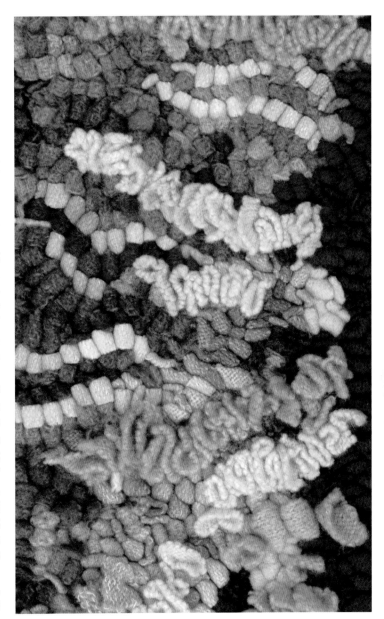

Detail of the tree.

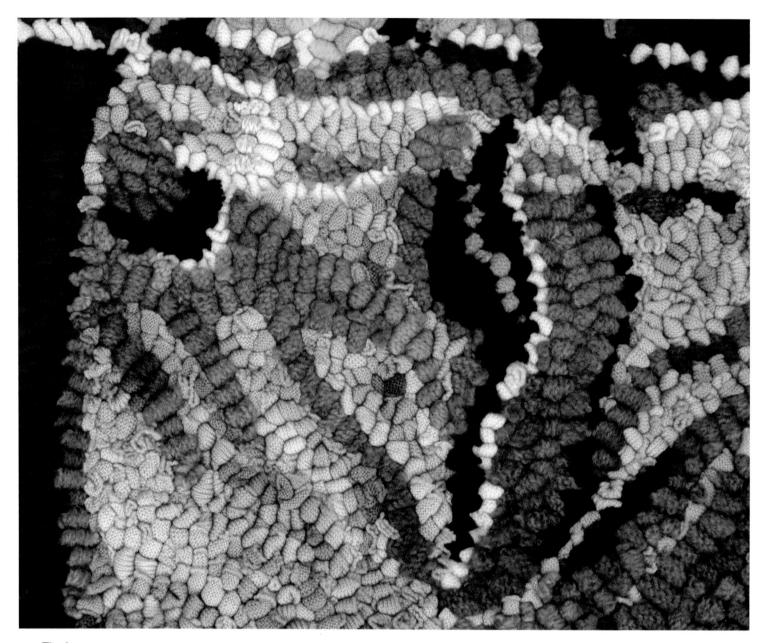

The jeans.

Heather used a wide variety of greens, browns and creams in the trees, all of them shades which are found in nature. Indeed, if you study a tree really closely you will observe all of these colors in it somewhere.

Heather loved living and working in Hurst. "The freedom, the silence, the darkness — all of these things inspired and supported me in my rug-making work. Les was working long hours in the baker's shop and my children were still very young — rug-making and walking the dogs in the heathery hills kept me going through some very difficult times."

The jeans are made of a variety of sweaters, all used "as is", but they look like faded indigo-dyed denim, so accurate was Heather's choice of colors.

The brass button above the zip, the button hole on the waistband, the belt loops and the zip are all clearly defined. Heather regrets that there is a variety of fabrics in the rug, that it is not pure wool, but it is standing the test of time very well apart from being a little faded. This is mostly the result of never having been used as a floor rug for walking on, of course.

Heather made this rug after leaving Hurst and making it brought back many happy memories. She said, "there are many reasons why I love living in the middle of Reeth, but there are also many reasons why I would love to be living my time in Hurst all over again. Not at the age I am now, you understand, but as I was then..." and, just for a moment, she drifts off into a memory.

My Little Bonnie

My Little Bonnie, fine-cut wool on white linen, 2004. 14 x 12 inches (35 x 30cm). *Collection of the artist*

Bonnie was the first Border Collie the Ritchies owned, having previously enjoyed the company of a variety of breeds of dog. She was a very intelligent dog, as will become apparent in *Paradise Garden* (Chapter 16) and she was devoted to Heather's husband, Les. She appears, lying under the bench in Les's workshop, in *Good Companions* (Chapter 15). This rug shows her connection to Hurst because it is based on a photo Heather took during the family's time there.

The Ritchie family adopted Bonnie as a puppy. Heather and Les still speak very fondly of Bonnie, even several years after her death, and this rug is very special to both of them. Bonnie was not really "little" — that is just Heather's affectionate term for her.

The original photo of Bonnie in the heather near Hurst. *Archives of the artist.*

"This rug is made on my favorite backing, white linen," says Heather, "and I made it in a class in America. I took a photo of Bonnie in the heather at Hurst to the class with me and I used that as my source material."

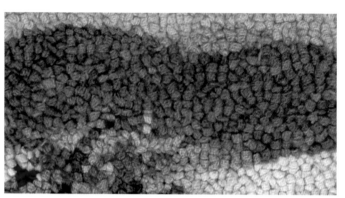

The colors in a sprig of heather in the foreground are echoed in the hills which roll away behind Bonnie.

Detail of the beautiful heather surrounding Bonnie.

Heather started the rug by completing Bonnie. "I did the heather around her by dotting in various shades of pink and purple, then I just filled in the spaces with the greens. That way of working always gives me a nice texture for flowers." The heather and the scenery behind Bonnie are created with wider-cut loops than the dog herself. "Bonnie is made with very fine strips, settings 3 and 4 on my cutter, which is as fine as you can get without the fabric shredding and dropping to bits on you," Heather explains.

"I made up the background using subtle colors for the distant hills because I wanted Bonnie to stand out." Bonnie is lying in the heather-covered moorland which surrounds Hurst with the landscape fading away almost to invisibility behind her. Even if the photo had showed darker hills behind Bonnie, Heather would have used light colors so that the dark-colored dog stood out clearly from the background.

Bonnie's face is finely executed with beautiful bright eyes but Heather is very modest about this rug, saying, "I wasn't too thrilled with Bonnie's face because I felt that there was some foreshortening of her nose. I should have added some shading to lengthen it. I did some sculpting, cutting into the pile to try to get the shape right. When I made a rug of my dog Fleet, later on, I did his face in profile. That was so much easier because I could get the nose right, but Bonnie's full-front face simply didn't work." She says that this was the first dog she tried hooking and she had not appreciated how hard it would be to get the nose right. Looking back, she feels that she should have used some shadow to correct the perspective problem.

Turning to Bonnie's body, she says, "I cut into some of these loops on her fur to get a feather effect because she was a very freckled dog and her fur was really thick. I used several shades of white and cream, grey and pale brown for her chest fur, and black and grey for her body. I think I captured the character of Bonnie in this rug — she was a wonderful dog."

Bonnie's face.

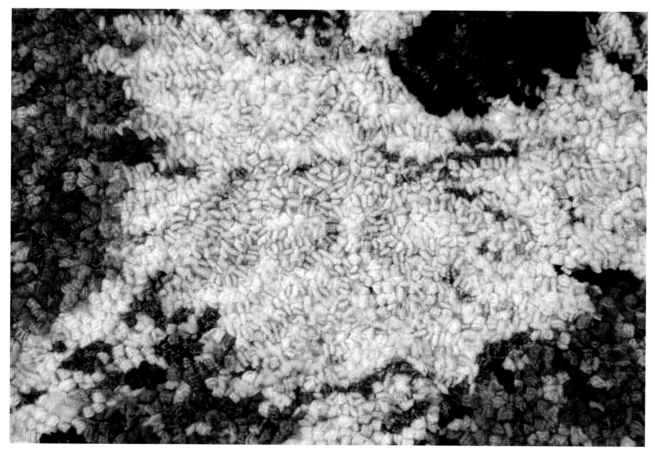

Bonnie's chest with its distinctive, flecked fur.

Fleet

Fleet, fine-cut wool on white linen, 2001. 30 x 20 inches (76 x 50cm). *Collection of the artist.*

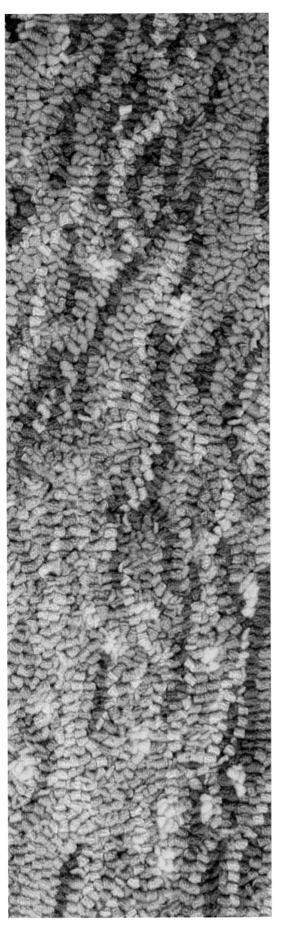

The third rug in this chapter shows the Ritchies' second Border Collie, Fleet. "This was a later rug, made sometime after *My Little Bonnie*," says Heather. "I've done several dog rugs after that one and I've been happier with them all because they're in semi-profile at least. It's much easier to get the shape of the nose in profile."

The rug is based on a photo taken by Heather which shows Fleet sitting in a grassy field. "I set up the photo so I could make the rug," she says. "I made him sit and stay in a field full of buttercups. In the rug they're just little dots of yellow, but you see whatever your eye wants to read into it and they represent buttercups quite well."

Heather has removed some of the clutter of vegetation from the background of the photo. "There was a lot of other stuff which I've left out — I just wanted to see him and the buttercups and simplifying the background really helps."

Fleet's fur, as represented in hooky, looks like it is being caught by the breeze: as a long-haired Border Collie, he pays regular visits to the canine beauty parlour to have the tangles, vegetation and dead fur removed from his coat. In the photo on which Heather based this rug, it looks like Fleet might just have had one of his regular treatments as his coat is clean, shiny and neat.

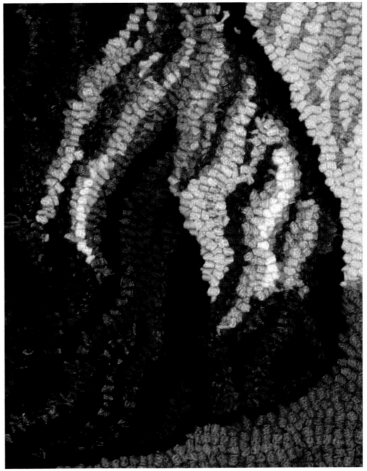

Buttercups in the grass around Fleet.

Fleet's shiny, clean fur catches the light.

Heather's original photo of Fleet. *Archives of the artist.*

Fleet's head.

The strips used to make *Fleet* are very fine, and some of them are pure white. "It's a problem to find this lovely white wool," says Heather. "Most of it is actually cream and this has been chemically treated to whiten it somehow. It's not often that I find white woollen fabric in the UK. I find it in the USA sometimes and then I hang on to it in case I want to do an animal or something which needs a real white."

This rug is made on a white linen backing and Heather has over-sewn the edges. She claims that it needs repairing, although any damage it has suffered can only have occurred in transit. Like most of Heather's rugs, *Fleet* regularly comes down off the wall to go with her to shows and talks.

Despite appearances, there was nobody out of shot to Heather's left attracting Fleet's attention while he posed for this photo. That may be where his attention is focussed, but Heather says that it was simply a question of making him sit still and taking lots of photos until she got the one she wanted, one in which his nose was in full profile. If your subject will not cooperate as readily as Fleet did (eventually), you might need to have someone or something attract their attention away from the camera. This tip is worth remembering if your chosen subject is a child or an animal. If they see you looking at them through a lens, they will come towards you and, while that might be a lovely photo, it may not be the best shot from which to make a rug.

This rug demonstrates the importance of feeling free to change elements in your source material which do not lend themselves to rug-making or which fail to make a useful contribution to the design. Showing that tangle of vegetation in the background might have made the rug a more truthful version of the photo, but that truth would not have contributed anything useful or beautiful to the design.

Heather has captured the eager anticipation which lights Fleet's deep brown eyes and they are even more clear in the rug than in the photo.

I had a couple of days in a class with Elizabeth Black, the famous rug-maker. She suggested the shadow beneath Fleet as a way to root him in the ground. She's a superb teacher and artist when it comes to animals in rugs. She guided me and told me about the colors to use, like not giving him a pink tongue when I did his face. I dyed some fabric and took it with me to her class so I had the colors for the eyes, for instance. It was marvellous to have her there to say, 'the shape of that eye isn't right' or whatever.

Timmy

Timmy, mixed media on even-weave Scottish hessian, 2001. 28 x 21 inches (71 x 53cm). *Collection of the artist*

The next rug features Timmy the cat, who is in the window in *Good Companions* (see Chapter 15) as well as beside the Aga on the top rug of *The Steps* (Chapter 10).

This charming rug is one of Heather's earliest experiments with mixed textures as well as mixed media, and Timmy has been given a beautiful and very real patchwork quilt from Heather's collection to lie on in his basket. The photo on which the rug was based shows that this generosity is typical of Heather; Timmy is lying on a warm and comfortable hooky rug with his head resting on a very labor-intensive patchwork quilt. Maybe Heather stumbled upon Timmy resting where he should not have been, but he looks very comfortable.

The Timmy in the rug looks younger, more of a kitten, so perhaps Heather is simply trying to justify and excuse allowing a cat such luxury by depicting him as a naughty kitten.

Heather's original photo of Timmy in the lap of luxury. *Archives of the artist.*

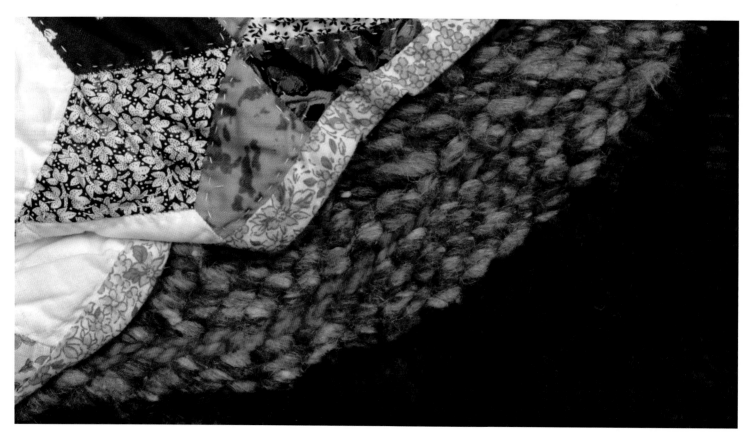

The basket is made of reverse hooky using yarn.

In the rug, Timmy's quilt is lining a wicker-work basket which is created using a very simple variant of hooky. The basket is hooked on the wrong side in reverse hooking, leaving extra-long spaces between the loops. The loops are kept short, but not too short: they must be secure.

This cockerel stands on reverse hooky soil made of a knitted woollen fabric.

The Cockerel — reverse hooking

This section of another rug, *The Cockerel*, shows the technique used in a small rug in conjunction with both conventional hooky and proddy. Here Heather did not want to obtain the same tight, neat basket-weave effect, so more of the raw edges are visible. A very narrow range of shades of pale green give this the appearance of rough, dry soil.

Naturally, this technique produces an uneven reverse to the rug, and Heather always covers the back of any piece of work which contains reverse hooky to reduce the possibility of damage. The rug also ends up thicker than normal because it has pile on the front and the reverse. As a result, it is not a suitable technique to include in a floor rug, because the uneven surface might be dangerous to walk on and the more prominent areas are much more vulnerable to wear. Heather says that *The Cockerel* was a sample piece to show mixed techniques; it contains hooky, proddy, reverse hooky and alternating colors in hooky. It has a backing to cover the reverse hooky loops and is made on hessian. "It's not great," says Heather with her usual modesty. "I made it a few years ago, and it is based on a design by Diana O'Brien. Her version was fantastic!"

Turning back to Timmy, the edge of his basket is created using locker stitch hooking. This is a simple and very effective technique in which a length of yarn or strip of fabric is caught in each of the loops that are pulled down quite tight to the backing. This produces a tunnel-like effect and makes the work very secure. It is the ideal way to use fleece that is prone to being caught and pulled, or as padding for loops of very fine fabric. Locker stitch is normally used in straight rows with the underlying locking on the front of the work.

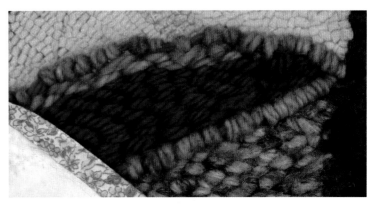

The edge of the basket is made using locker stitch.

Locker stitch: using a bodkin (or a large blunt needle) to pull the yarn through the loops. The technique can be used to secure loops of fabric or fleece.

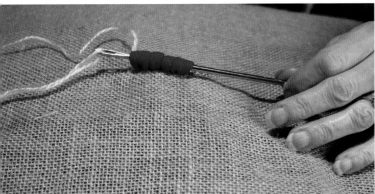

Timmy is hooked using a mixture of tabby shades — brown, cream, grey and black — and Heather has used a little more black to define the division between his toes as well as to outline his front leg where it embraces the quilt. She describes how this rug was created: "I hooked the parts of Timmy which were going to show and then I stitched the quilt around him." If she had created the whole of his body it would have led to too great a bulk of hooking behind the fabric quilt.

In contrast to the complexity of the foreground, the background of this rug is simple. Between Timmy and the corner of the plain deep brown wooden wall behind him stands a table lamp. The shade over the bulb is made of a semi-opaque material and the majority of the light is forced down onto Timmy. Some light is shining through the lampshade to show that it is a delicate shade of peachy pink. This shade could be made of glass or it could be pieces of delicate, thinly-layered, Capiz shell. Either way some of the light is falling, in yellow-cream beams, onto Timmy in the basket. You can see it reflected in the glossy light-reflecting fur on his back and rear leg. In the old days of energy-inefficient incandescent light bulbs, this was a simple way of providing cats with warmth; a warm cat tends to sleep and a sleeping cat is a happy cat.

Timmy's finely-detailed foot.

The spiral wooden lamp stand.

Heather points out a flaw in this rug: the backing in the area surrounding the wooden upright of the lamp is distorted. She says that the rug will not lie flat because she has "used fine flannel next to great heavy blankets" and that the hessian is too unforgiving to tolerate the tension this produces.

Linen, her favorite backing, would have withstood it much better, she says.

Using linen might also have prevented some of the damage the rug has suffered. As Heather points out, "this rug's got a bit battered with carrying it everywhere; everyone loves it so I take it to all my talks and shows. It's a thick and heavy rug: as well as the reverse hooky, there is some padding behind the quilting which I've stitched to the backing in places to hold it in the draped shapes around Timmy." It is worth remembering how heavy a large mixed-media rug can become, especially if you intend to hang it on the wall. (See Chapter 6, *Percival's Bus,* for more about hanging rugs.)

Some of the rays of light are caught in Timmy's fur.

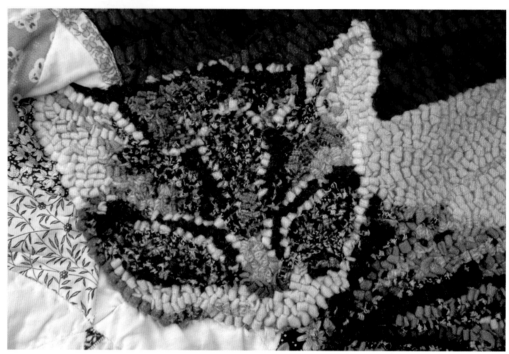

Timmy's contented tabby face.

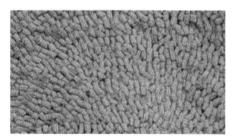

A section of the Capiz lamp shade.

Partly because of that padding and the texture of the basket and Timmy's fur, this is an almost three-dimensional rug that cries out to be touched as well as being delightful to look at. This is true of most of Heather's rugs, but Timmy looks so comfortable that it is hard to resist the temptation to reach out and stroke him. Heather encourages her blind and visually-impaired students in The Gambia (see Chapter 18, *Origins and Identity*) to use their hands to tell them where they are in their work and to work out what needs doing next. These students will need many years' practice before they can produce anything as glorious as the rugs in this chapter, but their simple hooky work is wonderful and is just as tactile as *Timmy.*

Bearing Gifts

Bearing Gifts, various cuts of wool on white linen, 2008. 29 x 23 inches (73 x 58cm), plus fringe. *Collection of the artist*

The final rug which relates directly to Hurst is *Bearing Gifts,* which Heather made to use as her Christmas card in 2008. It is an amalgamation of two photos, both of which were taken during the time the Ritchie family lived at Hall Farm, Hurst.

The photo that provides the background was taken by Laurence. It shows Chrissie emerging through the front door behind her mother. Heather is standing in the area cleared of snow by the local gamekeeper, Tony Williams, who had just dug a path to the Ritchies' front door. Deep snow fell during one night when Les was away at sea and Heather could not even open the front door. Luckily, Tony saw that they needed help and cleared the snow away. You can still see snow piled halfway up the window on the left. Although the photo was taken in the morning, Heather has set the scene in late afternoon so that she can have lighted windows and evening colors in the shadows falling on the snow.

Heather describes the house as she represented it in the rug. "Some snow has been blown by the wind up on to the front of the house, on to the porch and the window sills as well as the prominent bits of stone work. The porch had a side door and a window at the front so the light is falling on the snow."

Hall Farm, Heather's home in
Hurst, after a snow storm in 1992.
Courtesy of Laurence Ritchie

The lights are on inside the rug version of Hall Farm.

The second photo shows Heather clutching two young lambs, one under each arm. The stance of her body is typical of the pose taken when supporting such a weight—a farmer's wife who saw the rug identified with it immediately.

Heather with two strong lambs. *Courtesy of Laurence Ritchie.*

Each of the lambs' bodies is made of washed, un-spun fleece, a mixture of Swaledale and Wensleydale, and their legs and heads are dyed flannel and sweater.

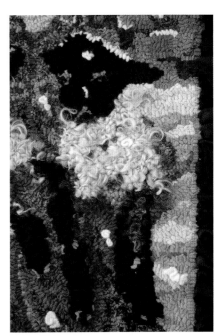

The lamb on the right: judging by the sharp contrast between the lambs' white fleece and their black faces and legs, these are probably Suffolks.

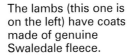

The lambs (this one is on the left) have coats made of genuine Swaledale fleece.

Heather's high-collared coat was actually a pale blue, but she changed it to green to distinguish it from her jeans. Luckily, she had a good selection of shades of green available, having dyed and over-dyed so many fabrics in the past. As always, Heather knew it was important that she created a real sense of the movement and shape brought to the clothes by her body beneath them as well as the weight and wriggling of the lambs pulling on the fabric of her coat. Another factor distorting her clothes is the wind, which was blowing over her as well as threatening to blow her over.

The wind is also blowing through Heather's hair. As she said, "it was no good doing your hair in Hurst. As soon as you set foot outdoors, woof! Your hair was almost blown away by the wind." She has replicated her wind-blown hair and added a halo of light around her head to make it stand out from the stone wall of the house behind her.

Heather's right leg is shaded in the original photo and she has added this detail to the rug. Her jeans reflect some of the light coming off the snow and the shading and folds of the fabric are very effective.

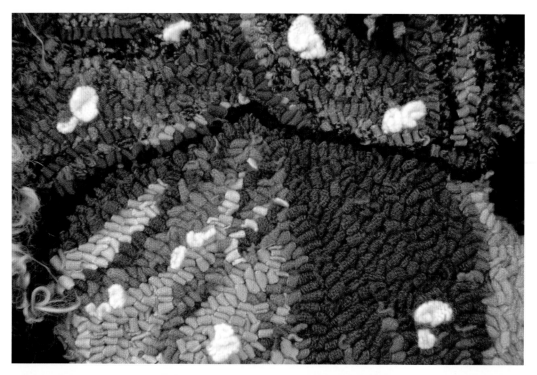

Heather's green jacket and dark jeans are being pulled by the weight of the lambs.

Heather's hair is very windblown, and it gives a strong impression of being lit from behind.

All the fabrics used in this rug are wool. "Because I made this rug for my Christmas card in 2008," says Heather, "I added some Christmas roses and holly. I just made little knots in some red yarn for the holly berries, then cut up a green sweater into double-ended leaf shapes and pulled the knots through them to make the clumps of leaves and berries at the same time. I made the Christmas roses in a similar way, using knots of gold ribbon." Christmas roses are available in a range of colors, but these white ones are the classic variety.

Heather says she is "quite happy" with this rug. Unlike *The Evacuees* (see Chapter 5), whose labels are made of embroidery nestling in the hooky, Heather has used running stitches to add the words "Hall Farm" to a piece of fabric that she has sewn to the porch. Here the letters are as clear and straight as the stone-carved letters above Hall Farm's real front door; in *The Evacuees* the letters are shaped by the loops they are sitting among.

The Christmas roses and holly in the bottom corner of the rug.

The white sign above the door is a tiny piece of white cotton: Heather has embroidered the letters.

When she was ready to finish the rug, Heather added a fringe all around the edge made of pointed strips of pure wool, Black Watch tartan cut on the cross. She put the strips in with a spring hook because their bulk was too great for a hook or prodder to manage. This edging feels almost like felt.

Using a spring hook: push the jaw under several threads of the backing and grip the proddy strip; pull the strip through both holes, making sure that it is evenly distributed; repeat the grip and pull, leaving only a small space between strips; the resulting proddy, all worked from the front of the rug.

Heather's daughter Chrissie, wearing ear muffs, stands beside the front door (just as in the original photo).

The actual finishing touch came when Heather was struck by the thought that she had never included snowflakes in any of the rugs she has made for use as Christmas cards. She decided to try adding some to see what they looked like. So, as she puts it, she "just prodded some little bits through so they curled up." Snowflakes may not curl, but they do clump together like this as they fall, and snow is the perfect finish to this gloriously happy rug.

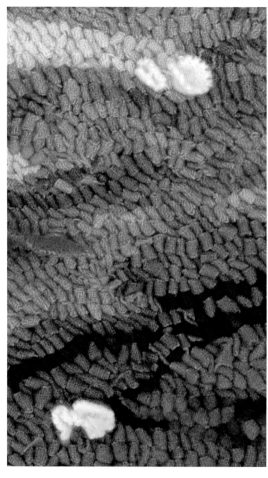

The snowflakes are all doubled up because they are made using the proddy technique.

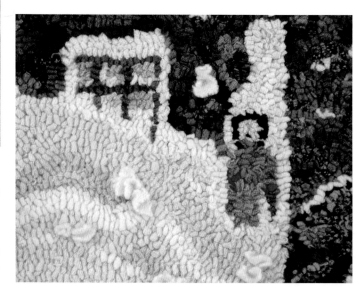

15

Good Companions

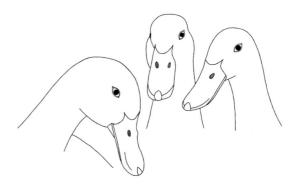

This rug shows Les, Heather's husband of over forty years, hard at work with his favorite materials, wood and metal, while the family's animals watch.

Les has been mentioned in several chapters of this book and he is a very important part of Heather's rug-making life. His involvement began when Heather expressed her dismay at having no option but to buy hooks from the United States. Les made a series of hooks for her in the 1980s, and when Heather commented that it would be very useful to have a stretcher frame, Les made one for her. Later he developed a lap frame for Heather before making some prodders. All of these items were greatly admired by Heather's rug-making friends as well as her students so Les, being a kind man, made some more for Heather to give away. Eventually, shops and craftsmen at home and abroad started asking for tools to sell and Les responded positively to these requests.

When he retired from life in Britain's Merchant Navy, Les became a full-time craftsman. Nowadays he is usually to be found working hard in his workshop, just as he is shown in this rug. He refers to his workshop as his "hut," his Sunderland accent making the word rhyme with the Received Pronunciation English (short vowel) "foot."

Les's hut stands at the top of Greencroft's garden, near the house, and it has one large window that faces roughly east. This gives Les a glorious, uninterrupted and inspiring view of Fremington Edge as he works. After spending much of his working life in ships' engine rooms far away from daylight, he really appreciates this view and often looks up at it during the day. Les manages to find inspiration rather than diversion in having such a wonderful sight to gaze upon as he works, with the sun falling on the rocks and plants of Fremington Edge standing high above Reeth.

A view from the garden of Greencroft towards Fremington Edge.

Good Companions, fine-cut wool on white linen, 2002. 28 x 20 inches (71 x 50cm). *Collection of the artist*

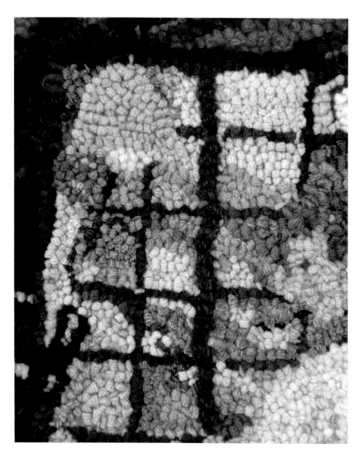

Heather has changed the layout of the hut slightly by giving it two small windows divided into panes by glazing bars, a useful shorthand way to indicate the presence of a window, and she has given both of those windows a view of Greencroft's garden. Once again, that is one of the joys of rug-making; you can tell whatever story you want to tell. Heather's choice was the right one as it would have been hard to give an adequate impression of Fremington Edge in such a small space. Dividing the window into panes and putting the garden behind them works very well.

The rug version of the window through which Les can (and does) admire the view.

Heather based this rug on a photo she took secretly while Les was working. "I peeped 'round the door when he wasn't looking," she says, "because I needed something to copy to get the body language right. I added the workshop background around him." She says that her main problem was getting the perspective right when there were so many straight lines. Les was unaware that Heather was working on this rug until it was finished, and she gave it to him for his birthday, although she promptly took it back to hang in her studio and to use in teaching sessions.

Les is smiling broadly as he stands in front of the lathe he uses to turn the wood from which he makes the handles of hooks and prodders. He is a happy man, contented in his work, and a smile comes naturally to him. He uses a variety of woods for the handles he turns, all of them obtained from sustainably managed forests. He has another lathe that he uses to make the ultra-smooth metal hooks or prodders, which are fixed to the handles with a brass ring or collet.

While he works, he listens to the radio and he has a phone close at hand to answer the many enquiries that come in about rug-making and Heather's classes

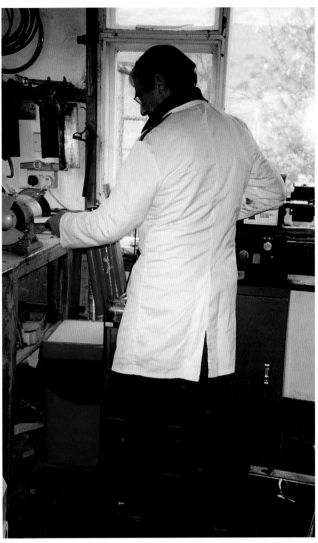

Les, hard at work, in a photo he wasn't aware Heather was taking. *Archives of the artist.*

Les in the rug, smiling and happy: Heather added his pipe!

Two saws, a bucket and two hoops hang from the ceiling, various containers and tools are housed on the shelves, and a pint of home-brewed beer stands in the bottom right corner.

The walls of Les's hut are covered with shelves and, like many men, he keeps a lot of things because "it will come in handy one day." A lot of these useful things are stored in jars and tins, and Heather has made the most of the opportunity this provides to show an array of brightly colored storage containers. Les always knows where an item is stored and he can nearly always find the solution to any domestic crisis somewhere in his hut.

or workshop sessions. He also takes calls from places that stock his tools, like the open-air museum at Beamish in County Durham. Les has smoked a pipe most of his adult life, but he seldom smokes in the house now. Although he often holds his pipe in his mouth as he works, he only lights it in the garden. He always has a mug of tea or coffee beside him because wood turning is dusty, thirsty work. If the weather is hot, he may replace the tea with a glass of ice-packed lemonade or a pint of home-brewed beer. All visitors to the Ritchies' home are invited to taste Les's beer, and everyone thoroughly enjoys it.

Hanging from the ceiling and stored on the shelves above and below the workbench are various tools, including saws, pliers, screwdrivers and chisels, and hoops for making rugs.

Leaning against the shelves just inside the door are a brush and shovel so that Les can tidy up after a day's work. There is a vacuum extractor that takes most of the dust away from the lathe as it runs, sending it into dust-proof bags in an adjacent shed, but some of the larger chips of wood fall onto the floor. Les is a very neat, tidy and methodical man and he keeps his hut as clean as he can. As he says, "you wouldn't want to eat your dinner off the floor, but that's not what a floor's for." Over his jeans Les is wearing a white knee-length work coat to protect his clothing.

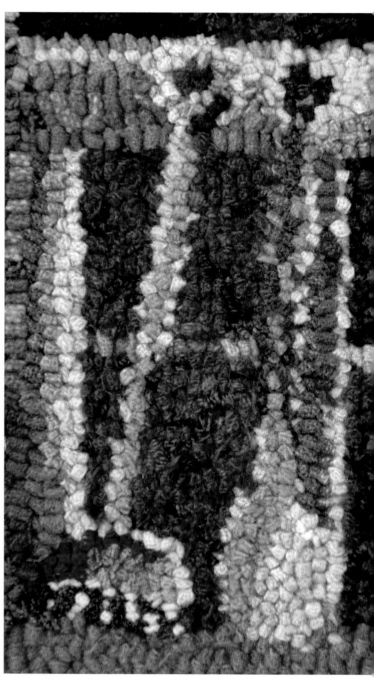

A brush and spade lean up against the workbench.

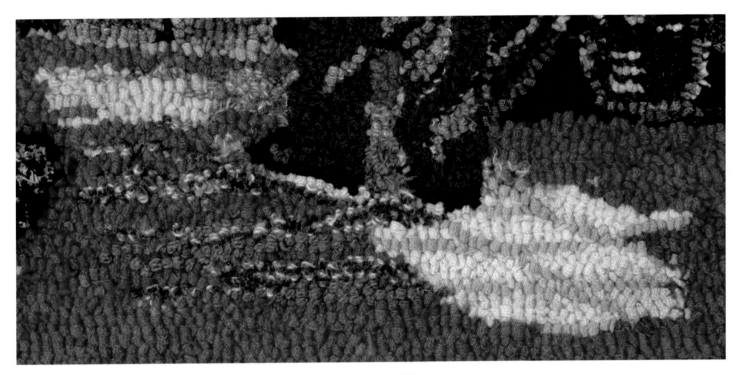

Les stands on a section of worn flooring between two patches of sunlight.

Light from the bulb overhead casts a patch of creamy yellow on the floor in front of the lathe and the sunlight entering through the window, with the pattern of the glazing bars casting a shadow in its brightness, does the same. This shows up the area of the wooden floor where Les's feet, walking between processes during the day, have worn away the painted surface.

For most of the year while Les is working, the door to the hut is propped open to help ventilate the air. Despite the pump that removes most of the dust, the air still needs to be refreshed.

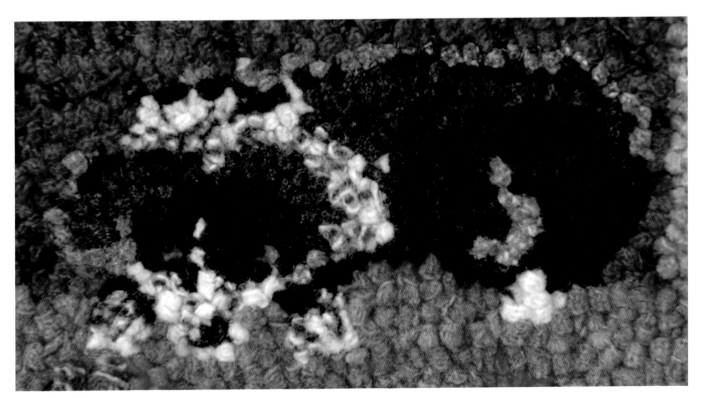

Faithful, patient Bonnie lies under the bench, waiting for her master to finish his day's work. She's not asleep, and seems to be watching the hens and ducks.

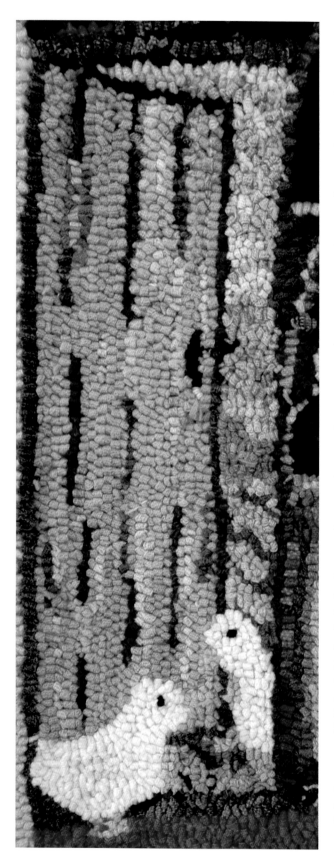

Sadly, several of the animals featured in this rug are no longer members of the Ritchie household. The first of these now-departed friends, lying under Les's workbench waiting for her master to finish work for the day, is Bonnie the faithful Border Collie. Bonnie was a natural at the task Border Collies were bred for, controlling sheep. The Ritchies adopted her when they lived at Hurst and she, in her own turn, adopted a shepherd, a local farmer who would take her out when he tended his sheep. He did not need to call round to collect Bonnie, he simply whistled for her from his own farmyard a little distance away and she would run like the wind across the intervening fields to join him.

The tweedy grey fabric Heather has used for Bonnie's muzzle and shoulders echoes her natural coloring precisely. Heather is very pleased with this likeness and says that she feels she has captured the essence of Bonnie here. She compares it with the foreshortened nose of *My Little Bonnie* (see Chapter 14) and the version in *Paradise Garden* (see Chapter 16), both of which must look wonderful to everyone else. Perhaps her success is due to the fact that this is Bonnie in her favorite place. As Heather says, "Bonnie wanted nothing more than to be with Les, and she lay under his bench, sleeping quietly, all day."

Heather is pleased with the way she has portrayed the battered old door to the hut. You can see the layers of paint lifting off to reveal other colors beneath. Standing in the doorway are two sturdy white ducks, while three fine brown hens have made it all the way into the hut. Heather says that these birds, which always had completely free range in the Ritchies' garden, were always wandering in and out of the door. At the time of writing, the garden of Greencroft is less busy than it was, with only one white hen and one white duck wandering around, grubbing up the soil in search of worms and other juicy morsels to supplement their diet of mixed grain and layers' mash. At one time there were six of each and they laid plenty of eggs, some of which could occasionally be found in the nest boxes in the hen house.

The ducks are standing by the door, whose flaking paint reveals earlier color schemes.

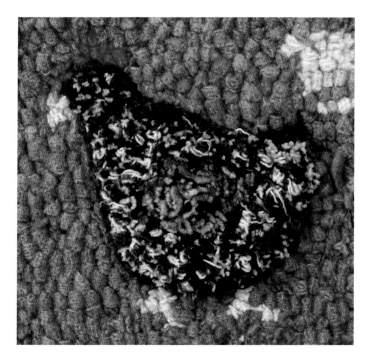

A superbly-executed speckled hen made using Waldoboro technique.

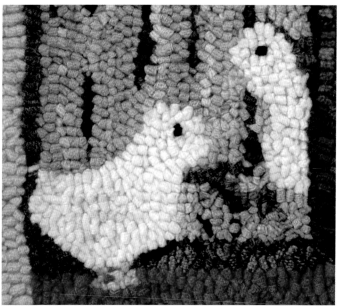

The one remaining hen often wanders into the kitchen, presumably looking for extra-delicious scraps of food. As will be shown in *Paradise Garden* (Chapter 16), this hen gets a good supply of spilled wild bird food as well as her own special diet, so perhaps she is looking for company when her claws tick across the stone floor of the kitchen.

The ducks are the white Aylesbury variety with yellow bills and black eyes. The hens are made of fine-cut tweedy fabrics in a raised-and-cut Waldoboro technique. This is hooky worked densely close, then cut and sculpted to produce a soft, feathery surface, slightly proud of the background. Astonishingly, Heather says of these hens, "they're not very good and I'd do better now."

Zack, the black and white cat, is sitting on the window sill outside the hut alongside his friend Timmy, just as both of them are seen sitting on opposite sides of the Aga in the final rug of *The Steps* (see Chapter 10). Zack was a cat whose nine lives had been used up by accidents. He had only one eye and part of an ear was missing. He joined the Ritchie household when they lived at Hurst and he probably fought with more than one fox in his time. Zack was a real character who thought nothing of falling out of a tree or a window, and he genuinely loved people, especially people with tin openers who were obviously about to feed him.

Timmy (who also features in a rug included in *My Animals and Other Family Members,* see Chapter 14) was a large brown tabby cat with an excellent, friendly nature. He had an inviting tabby tummy and would sink all of his teeth and claws into your hand as you tickled it — typical cat behavior. Heather has portrayed him as a grey tabby to make him more visible against the background where his natural brown shades would simply blend in.

The two ducks standing in the door appear to be having a conversation.

Timmy and Zack are sitting on the window sill outside, watching Les at work.

Heather added the title and her initials across the bottom of the rug.

Les's hard-working hands hold three of his carefully-crafted tools. *Courtesy of Nicky Rogerson*

It is very unusual for Heather to make the title an integral part of a rug, and she has signed this one with her initials too, although both of them have now faded into the background a little. These animals really were good companions to Les who returned the compliment; each of them content to let the others get on with whatever task they were undertaking in peace.

Les works long hours in his hut, every day of the week and all the year round. Now that Heather is working through Rug Aid to teach rug-making to underprivileged people, Les is even busier making tools and frames for her to take and leave behind at no cost to the trainees at the workshops in Africa. These are Les's generous contribution to Rug Aid's work, and Rug Aid is very grateful to him for his support.

Because he has made tools for Heather for so many years, Les has experimented with a variety of handle shapes ending up with four that he makes regularly.

Hooks and prodders

As you can spend many happy hours rug-making it is important that the hooks and prodders you use have handles that feel comfortable in your hand — not just when you first pick up the tool but also at the end of a long and productive session.

Handle shapes vary considerably: the slim parallel-edged handle, which suits people who like to hold a hook in the same way that they would hold a pencil, can be used for every size of tool from the very finest hook up to the largest prodder. A broader handle fits inside the palm of the hand and can accommodate a medium or large hook or prodder.

A selection of tools in various woods.
Courtesy of Nicky Rogerson

The large handle fills the palm of the hand and Heather normally finds this shape very comfortable to work with over long periods. When her rug-making hand aches she often uses an easy-grip handle that Les developed for her. This handle can be fitted with any size of hook or prodder and Heather finds it a supremely comfortable shape to use, even during long rug-making sessions.

Heather calls the tool she uses most often a "bent hook." By altering the angle at which she holds her wrist, it has removed some of the stress that led to serious damage.

If any talk of damage worries you, please remember that Heather has worked in rug-making for over 35 years and spent most of those years not even thinking about her wrists and hands, let alone their long-term future. She is keen that you should avoid the problems she has encountered, which is why she mentions the difficulties she faces. Heather does not want to put you off taking up this rewarding hobby — she would just like to encourage you to think more carefully about the way you work than she did.

It is important to use more than one handle shape during a working week to avoid the danger of repetitive strain injury. Rug hooks are not expensive and they can be very beautiful. If you can afford to have a variety of handles, your hands and wrists will thank you for it. Poor use can even have an impact on your arms and shoulders, even your neck (as Heather will attest).

Three large-handled tools, one with a medium hook and two with large hooks. *Courtesy of Nicky Rogerson*

A fine bent hook and three pencil-grip tools, one with a medium hook and two with large hooks. *Courtesy of Nicky Rogerson*

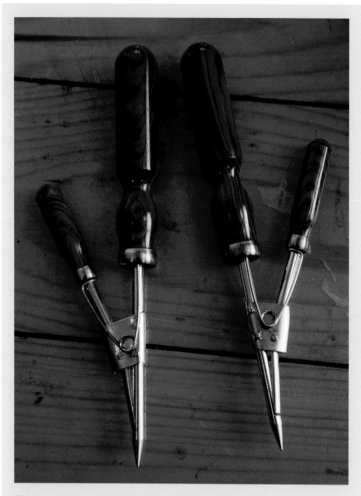

Two spring hooks. *Courtesy of Nicky Rogerson*

The spring hook is a tool that is used only for proddy work. You use it to pull a strip through from the back of the rug to the front, the reverse of the normal way of working proddy. Heather used a spring hook for the border around *Bearing Gifts* (in Chapter 14, *My Animals and Other Family Members*) and the technique is illustrated there.

Les developed all-wood tools for use when Heather teaches in Durham Gaol where metal tools are forbidden. The wooden hook (shown in the box on page 152) has a slim, pencil-type handle while the prodder is a purpose-built version of the improvised wooden rug-making tools our grandmothers might have used, such as an old peg or the handle of an old wooden spoon.

If possible, it is a good idea to try experimenting with as many different handle shapes as you can find. Ask every rug-maker you know if you can borrow their favorite tool for a few minutes to see how it feels in your hand; you will very soon know if it is likely to suit you.

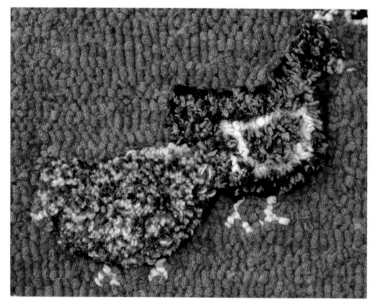

Two Waldoboro hens.

Take care!

It is very easy to slump as you work, so take care over your posture. Try not to bend from the upper back or neck, but do not lean too far forward. Make an effort to be body-conscious as you work, observing areas of tension and adjusting your stance to alleviate them.

Make sure the light you work by is as good as possible and remember, as Heather says, that nothing beats natural daylight. Experimentation is the key to finding a source of artificial light which suits your pocket as well as your eyes. Check out the various types of light used by artists in other media and ask your creative friends what suits them.

Remember, you are making rugs, not rheumatism; and eye-pleasers, not eye strain!

16

Paradise Garden

This large rug started life as one small piece of hessian and then, exactly like Heather's beautiful garden in Reeth, it just grew. The rug's focus, the woman sitting on the bench, is Heather's mother, Eleanor May Robson, née Milburn. Heather copied her mother's likeness from the last picture she took of her before she died, at the age of 95, in 1998. In the photo Eleanor May is sitting at the foot of the steps in Greencroft's garden.

Greencroft's garden was revamped soon after the family moved in. Following her normal habit of thinking about other people's comfort before her own convenience, Heather made sure that the newly-built steps were very shallow so that her mother could go up and down them easily. The garden was originally little more than a simple grassy bank running down to a stone boundary wall. Heather saw the garden's potential and very quickly transformed that plain green slope into an abundance of color and form. Green has always been one of Heather's favorite colors, but she does not like plain, flat green — or any other flat color — in a garden or a rug.

Eleanor May Robson sits in the garden of Greencroft with her good friend Bonnie. *Archives of the artist*

One of Heather's hens picks up spilt seed under the bird table in Greencroft's garden, May 2009.

Paradise Garden, mixed cuts and fabrics on even-weave Scottish hessian, 1999. 42 x 32 inches (106 x 81cm) *Collection of the artist*

Now, fifteen years after the planting activity which transformed it, Greencroft's garden features a great variety of trees and shrubs. They have deliberately been kept quite low to avoid obscuring the view of Fremington Edge, and most of them are festooned at head height with feeders for the flocks of wild birds that enjoy the conditions there. Outside the glazed doors, which lead from the kitchen into the garden, is a wonderful array of different types of feed container. Because it offers such a variety of foods, this feeding station attracts a range of different birds, including the hen that scurries around beneath it looking for spilled seed.

Eleanor May as she appears in the rug.

Eleanor May is sitting on the bench which Heather placed, solely for her mother's comfort, at the bottom of the steps. Heather's dog, Bonnie, is sitting at Eleanor May's feet in the rug, although she is standing in the photo. Eleanor May was very fond of Bonnie, who returned the sentiment in typical doggy fashion, and they often sat together in this spot watching the hens. Eleanor May visited Heather almost every day and she always came to lunch on Sunday, sitting in the garden with Bonnie afterwards if the weather allowed.

The rug is named after a piece of music by Delius, *The Walk to the Paradise Garden*. Heather's brother Keith chose this title because, as well as delighting in Heather's garden, their mother had a real love of all things musical. She shared this love with her late husband, Victor, (they met at a musical event) and they passed it on to their children and grandchildren.

Close-up of Eleanor May's head with a favorite blue scarf tied under her chin.

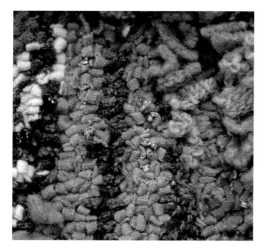

Tall spikes of mauve and blue flowers, enlivened with a hint of glitz.

Heather says, "I added a huge amount of detail in the garden around my mother and it was a really fun rug to work on." Except for the stylized flowers and Eleanor May, most of the fabrics used in this rug are recycled. Eleanor May and the big flowers are dyed fine wool flannel.

Eleanor May's favorite color was blue, and Heather has simply copied the photo when creating her mother's clothes That is one part of the jizz, the body language, that tells you this is Eleanor May. Heather says, "that's what I play on. As long as I can get the distinctive shape and color of someone's body, the person is there." She claims that this is not a good likeness of Bonnie but admits that, just like in *Christmas Carols* (Chapter 9), she decided to leave that part of the rug alone once it was finished.

As well as regular hooky, the rug is made with cut and uncut high loops and proddy. The rug includes a dizzying mixture of textiles: flannel, ribbon, scarves, glitzy fabrics, evening tops, blankets, thick and thin yarn, sweaters, cross-cut fabrics, velvets, embroidery threads, carpet thrums, dyed blankets, tweed skirts and, Heather's favorite, un-spun fleece. "I've used all sorts of different stuff in the rug," says Heather, claiming "I didn't really plan it."

An area of mixed flannel, yarn and other textiles, just to the right of the path.

Proddy

Like hooky, proddy uses a series of strips of fabric but proddy strips are much shorter and, usually, somewhat wider than hooky strips. The historic dales' size for a proddy strip is about two inches (5cm) long by ½ inch (12mm) wide, and two traditional methods were used to measure the required length. Either a long strip would be wrapped around a matchbox several times before cutting through it, or the (adult) rug-maker's index finger would provide the measurement needed to cut a piece from a long strip. Consistency of length is more important than precise measurement, and using one method or the other would lead to strips of even lengths.

If Heather is using mixed fabrics in a proddy rug she will use mixed widths too. This means cutting thick blankets into the normal strips, ½ inch (12mm) wide, while any sweaters she is including in the same piece will be cut to twice that width. She folds these wide strips in half before prodding them to balance the thickness of the blanket strips.

If you are using tweeds in a proddy rug, you need to take care not to cut the strips too narrow. When you push your prodder against such a strip it is likely to disintegrate as the prodding tool pushes it through the backing. This is frustrating and makes a terrible mess.

Proddy strips are pushed through the backing, one at a time, working from the reverse if you are using a simple prodder. If you are right-handed, that hand will hold the prodder on the top and your left hand will manipulate the strip underneath.

A sample of a (mostly) proddy mat which clearly shows that each short piece of fabric has two flying ends on the front.

Heather works on the edge of a proddy mat, prodding through the two layers of hessian.

A prodder is a piece of wood or metal (or metal with a wooden handle) ending in a blunt point. Rug-makers of old would simply use broken keys or pegs from the washing line that had been shaped and blunted to removed any areas which might snag on the fabric. (See *Good Companions*, Chapter 15, for examples of prodders.)

Apart from drawing your design on the reverse of your backing, there is one vitally important respect in which the process of transferring your design for a proddy rug differs from hooky. If you are including lettering or objects that are obviously right- or left-handed, you must draw them backwards. Obviously, this does not apply to symmetrical abstract patterns and it may not be vital if your design features flowers and/or animals. It might not apply to figures, faces, buildings and similar items if you have invented the design, but it is important that you do remember it when it does matter.

To cut your strips, you can follow the same basic methods as for hooky: these are explained in *The Evacuees* (see Chapter 5). It is not normally appropriate to use a strip cutting machine unless you happen to have one with a very wide cutting wheel.

If you choose to use a grid and a cutting wheel to cut long strips, you can use the same method to cut your long strips into short pieces for proddy if you take care to keep the fabric steady under the grid. You can also wrap long strips around a grooved rod which will allow you to cut even-sized pieces quickly using scissors.

Just as you start and stop a hooky strip in the same hole, so you revisit the previous hole with the first leg of each proddy strip, although each proddy strip covers a wider area on the reverse than is covered by a hooky strip.

Because of the much looser pile, it is hard to make accurate pictorial rugs using proddy on its own, but it is always possible to use proddy to produce a particular effect as part of a hooky rug, as Heather has done in *Paradise Garden*. Heather mostly uses simplified designs (and often sticks to geometric patterns or random color mixes) when creating an entirely proddy rug.

Mixed textiles and very different colors add great interest to this section of the rug.

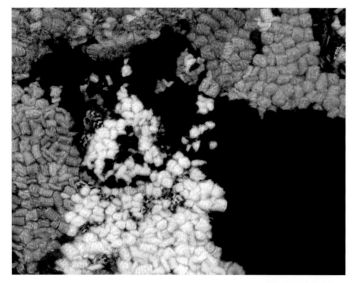

Sadly, Eleanor May developed age-related macular degeneration. This is a relatively common condition whereby older people lose vision at the center of the retina. The resulting blind spot means you cannot see the thing you look at directly, only things that are slightly off the center of your gaze. According to Heather, Eleanor May watched every wedding in Reeth but, after losing this crucial part of her vision, if she could see the bride's face she could not see her bouquet at the same time.

Some time after her husband Victor's death in 1972, and not long after they came to the dale, Eleanor May moved into an older person's flat in Reeth. Eventually her failing sight meant that she was forced to move into a residential home in nearby Richmond. Heather said that, initially, she did not want to go but she loved it and had a lot of fun when she was finally persuaded to move, for her own safety and Heather's peace of mind. There was a regular religious service in the home that Eleanor May enjoyed, joining in with the hymns she knew well enough to sing entirely from memory.

Bonnie must have missed Eleanor May when she moved to Richmond. This intelligent Border Collie had joined the Ritchie household as a puppy when they lived at Hurst. When Bonnie died, Heather and Les buried her in the garden she had loved so much.

Some areas of this rug, particularly Eleanor May and Bonnie, are worked in fine flat loops to keep the details clear. Looking across the figure of Eleanor May, the tall proddy and cut loop greenery behind her looks like a jungle in comparison to the orderly area surrounding her.

Close-up of Bonnie, the fourth time she has appeared in a rug in this book.

A view across the area of the rug which features Eleanor May, showing how the proddy work stands proud of the hooky.

Heather says, "my mother loved flowers, so in this rug I've surrounded her with some of her favorites, those big white daisies and rich purple lavender." Heather has created these beautiful flowers and those in the wider garden beyond the bench using a variety of fabrics and techniques.

This rug started growing during a rug-making class on gardens that Heather attended in Canada. She knew in advance exactly what kind of rug she wanted to make, and to guide her work she took the photo of her mother who had not long since died. However, as is the norm in many rug-making classes in North America, each student was given a piece of hessian with the same pre-printed design. Heather was not able to alter this design or work on a different rug, so she grumpily hooked the same pattern as the other participants. "I was the student from hell!" she says of herself.

But "waste not, want not" Heather enabled this reluctantly-completed piece of class work to take on a whole new lease on life when she got home. Back in England, she decided to include it in a much larger rug.

She extended that small piece of hessian by adding more backing above and below it as well as on both sides. The fantasy flowers she had created in class became just one component of this fabulous garden. The join between sections is barely visible on the reverse, except in the area just below Eleanor May's feet. Although the flowers are not her original design, she feels that they work well in the rug.

In the class, the students had been required to fill in the area between the flowers with flat color, and one of the first things Heather did after the class was to pull out that part of her work. She replaced the original filling with a variety of textures to represent other plants as well as flat hooking to introduce the garden path. This is a clever design element that draws the eye from the foreground flowers to the figures behind them.

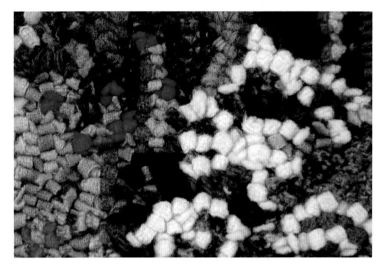

Big white floppy Michaelmas daisies were amongst Eleanor May's favorite flowers, so Heather included plenty of them.

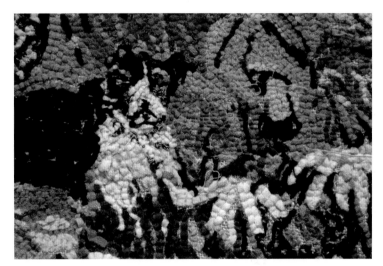

This section of the reverse of the rug shows how carefully Heather worked to join the small piece of hessian to the larger piece she needed to complete the rug. It also shows just how neatly and close together she works her rows of hooky.

A path is a very effective means of leading the eye into a picture, and this path is a beautiful one to tread as you walk into *Paradise Garden*.

Tall vertical flowers alongside some flannel hooky just to the left of Eleanor May's bench seat.

Eleanor May's favorite daisies stand just in front of the bench seat, which is hooked in three shades of brown to give the uprights a three-dimensional appearance.

The part of the rug Heather worked on in the class is copyrighted, but Heather's additions are her own designs, hence the absence of photos of all but tiny parts of those fantasy flowers.

Heather tells a funny story about this rug. She says, "my mother didn't leave Great Britain until she was 80 when she flew to Norway to visit my brother, and she was terrified. She never went anywhere else after that. But, since she died, she's been everywhere I have taken this rug, including Australia, Canada and the USA. She even went into the men's toilets at Heathrow airport with me. It's all grey outside there, the signing is unclear and the lighting isn't that great either. I was late for my plane and desperate to go to the loo so I just ran through a door with my mother under my arm. I can tell you that we ran out again pretty quickly!"

17

The Mat-making Group and Bolton Castle

community mat-making and teaching rug-hooking

The Mat-making Group

The Mat-making Group, mixed cuts and fabrics on white linen, 2000. 28 x 15 inches (71 x 38cm). Private Collection. *All photos of this rug are used courtesy Wayne Carroll.*

The first rug in this chapter is the only one in this book that Heather no longer owns. Barbara "Bobbie" True, who ran the Arrow Rock Rug Camp, admired the rug when she saw it in a class Heather taught at the Woolley Fox Rug School run by Wayne and Barb Carroll. Bobbie's husband Bill bought it for his beloved wife and Wayne took these photographs of the rug on Heather's behalf when he visited the Trues. Following Bobbie's untimely death in June 2009, the rug is now in Bill's care.

This mat is based on a photo that is currently in the archives of the Swaledale Museum in Reeth. The photo was included in an article that once formed part of an exhibition in the museum. Heather did not know the photo was there until very recently, and all she had to work from was a photocopy made in the 1980s. The dark and unclear image at the bottom of Heather's photocopy shows a group of older women sitting around a frame and working on a proddy rug.

The original photograph. *Courtesy of The Swaledale Museum, Reeth*

Frames and hoops

Stretcher frame

The rug in the previous chapter, *Paradise Garden*, is almost the largest in this book, and Heather used a stretcher frame while working on it. When a rug is as large (and correspondingly as heavy) as *Paradise Garden*, a frame provides some relief from the physical burden of its weight as well as putting the backing under an even tension as you work. Large frames also allow two or more people to work on a rug at the same time.

A stretcher frame has a strip of fabric (usually carpet tape) fixed to the bars on two edges. You sew the backing to this and wind it around one bar before tightening the mechanism on the sides that holds those bars apart. As you work, you wind the worked area of backing around the furthest bar, keeping it under even tension at all times.

This medium-sized domestic stretcher frame shows how the sides are adjusted to suit the rug.

Hoop

Heather sometimes uses a hoop, if she is working on a fine pictorial rug, while traveling for instance. Rug hoops differ from tapestry hoops in that they have a longer screw to accommodate the greater thickness of the backing and the pile.

Lap frame

Heather prefers to use a frame for proddy mats, as they enable the work to be held taut. This is important as proddy mats are heavy and the frame takes the weight and keeps the backing flat. Proddy is heavier than hooky because there is often more fabric — the pile is longer — and Heather's preference is to use a stretcher frame. A "confetti-mix" proddy mat (ie a traditional unpatterned rug made by using random strips) the size of a fireside rug needs about 18lbs (a little over 8 kilos) of fabric. Heather says, "I use a lap frame for ease but I have students who prefer not to use a frame at all, so this is not a hard and fast rule."

A frame is particularly useful if you are working on a proddy rug because each strip covers more of the backing and there is a possibility that over-tensioning the strips could distort the backing.

Overall, Heather prefers to work on a lap frame, which she finds practical and useful for most rugs. A lap frame is small enough to be portable and has a shelf beneath the working area to store scissors and spare hooks. With a strip of carding comb around the edge, your work is held very still, but can be re-positioned easily without damaging the backing.

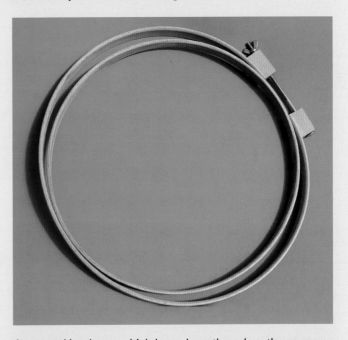

A rug-making hoop which has a long thread on the screw.

This lap frame provides a place for storing scissors and other tools while the rug is held firmly in place by the gripper strips around the top.

Heather knows the names of all of these women. On the left are Ada Stones, Jenny Banks, Edna Waller and Angela Stones. Marjory Hutchinson is at the head of the table and the ladies on the right are Martha Peacock, Annie Peacock, Marjory Stones, Nellie Reed and Nellie Hird.

The first part of the article (which formed a display with the photo) is missing, but what is left reads: "...and cloth remnants to produce a warm deep pile rug, and of course while away the long winter nights!" It continues:

The first task was to cut the cloth into small pieces (clippings, about two stone [12.7kg] in weight for a full-sized rug), keeping the colors separate for patterning. Then the hessian backing was sewn onto the stretcher bars of the frame, one end being rolled round the bar leaving about 2' [61cm] ready for working. The stretcher bars were then pegged to the side bars, pulling the hessian taut for prodding. The clippings were then prodded through the hessian with a wood or metal prodder,

The faces of the women in the center of the group.

The women on the right-hand side of the rug.

each end of the clipping through a separate hole and pulled tight from underneath (the front or face of the rug). As the work progressed the finished end would be rolled round one stretcher bar and more hessian released from the other. When the prodding was completed the bare hessian border was turned back under and hemmed in tidily. Smaller rugs often had cotton back linings.

Beneath the picture, the text reads:

Sadly very few proddy rugs are made in today's affluent television watching days. Our photo features the Methodist Ladies of Arkengarthdale making a full size rug to raise funds for the Chapel at the Annual "Sale of Work" a few years ago.

This rug is included here, despite its current distance from its maker in Reeth, because it is such a glorious illustration of the art of community mat-making. Heather has been instrumental in bringing a number of community mats to life in the past, and in recent years has nearly always been working on or planning a community mat-making project.

Reeth Village Hall, just over the road from Heather's home, houses a spectacular example which was made in 1999 by old hands and new rug-makers working together under Heather's guidance. Just along Swaledale, towards Richmond, another large example of a community rug made with Heather's help hangs on one wall of the twelfth century Marrick Priory. And the Durham Clayport Matters have a beautiful and slightly more portable example, which Heather helped to design, incorporating ideas that were suggested by members of the community that made it.

Heather's version of the picture is not intended to represent the hard-working ladies completely accurately because, despite knowing their names, she did not know them personally (unlike the men in *The Reeth Parliament*, Chapter 12). However, this rug is linked to that one because, as Heather puts it, "the men are sitting around putting the world to rights while the women get on and do something worthwhile."

The rug is an example of Heather's ability to introduce color into a monochrome image. The cardigans around this frame are bright and cheerful, and it is easy to imagine their wearers knitting them at the fireside during the long dark winter evenings.

Several of the ladies are wearing spectacles. Heather found these very challenging because they involve a straight line joined to a curve. Making those two very different shapes look realistic in hooky, while retaining recognizably human features beneath them, is quite a feat.

The ladies' hair presented Heather with the kind of challenge she really enjoys, and the results are wonderful. Compare these heads of hair to those in *Christmas Carols* (Chapter 9) to see just how imaginative Heather can be with hair. There is yarn and plenty of different types of fleece as well as one flannel head of hair. The fleece is from Swaledale and Wensleydale sheep, dyed as well as natural. The completely plain background permits each head to stand out clearly. Heather has only used dark lines to distinguish where faces overlap in a few places.

The two women nearest the front are both holding real prodders in their hands. These are scaled-down versions of Les's famous handiwork and, as well as looking fabulous, they bring a wonderful three-dimensional depth to the rug.

By far the most eye-catching part of the rug is the mat the ladies are working on. It is a riot of color and texture and is fascinating for being a proddy mat made, in part, using hooky. The plain brown hooky-hessian surface of the mat is visible at the edges where the women are resting their forearms. The central strip is almost completely covered with proddy strips waiting to be used.

But of course they have been used, in that they have been included in this rug. What is more, the proddy strips that the rug shows as having been used are made of hooky. As Heather might say, if you sat her down and made her think about it really hard, "it's enough to make your head spin!"

Heather has deliberately used the same fabric cut to both hooky lengths (14 inches [35.5cm]) and proddy lengths (two and a half inches [6.3cm]) to create this effect. Look for the same fabric and you will find it — the bluish mauve and the dusky pink are the easiest to spot, but there are others. Both the long hooky and short proddy strips are scaled, just like the prodders, but while the proddy strips are

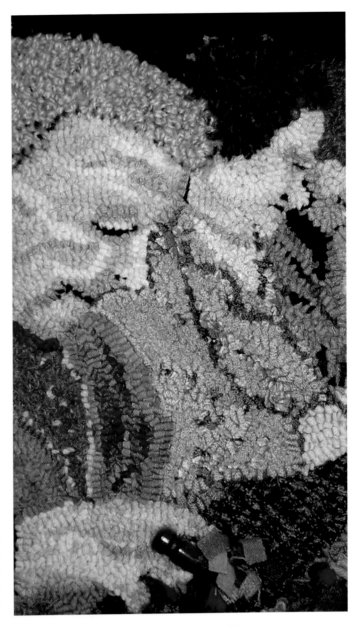

The two women on the left-hand edge of the rug.

The prodders and the "completed" proddy area in the foreground of the rug.

The photo taken at Bolton
Castle which inspired the rug.
Courtesy of Gene Shepherd

A small section of the tree in
the top left area of the rug.

slightly narrower and shorter than usual to fit the size of the women and their tools, the hooky strips are slightly wider so that they resemble the wider proddy strips of the finished rug. It really is "enough to make your head spin!"

Although the women are hard at work, they will also be chatting of course. It looks like the fourth woman from the left has her mouth open. Is her comment rug-related, is she asking for a particular color of strip perhaps, or is she passing on some gossip? Who is to say, and what does it matter? That is one of the joys of a pictorial rug — you can bring to it more or less whatever you want to bring and spin whatever tale you want about the folk it portrays.

Bolton Castle

The second rug in this chapter does not portray real people, but it does show a real place. This is part of the garden of Bolton Castle in Wensleydale, a little over four miles (6.4km) south of Reeth and the other side of a stretch of wild and windy moor.

This rug was inspired by a photo that Gene Shepherd, the noted American rug-maker, took on one of his visits to England. Heather enjoys taking her visitors to this lovely place, which is on the western edge of a village called Castle Bolton. Bolton Castle was built between 1378 and 1399 by Richard le Scrope, whose descendants still own the building. Mary Queen of Scots was held captive in the castle for six months, from mid-1568, and it suffered some damage during the English Civil War (1642-1651).

Heather, Gene and Gene's wife Marcia spent a happy few hours at this very ancient and almost magical place, including taking tea in its café and having a good wander round its beautiful garden. At one point, Gene took this photo of the view.

Gene and Marcia were staying with Heather during one of the Reeth Rug Retreats that Heather runs with Cilla Cameron. During this annual event, held every September, Heather always takes a class and there are two guest teachers. This particular year it was Gene's turn to teach a class.

Many of Heather's students come to the residential school for more intensive instruction. During the writing of this book, she retired from local authority teaching in Durham and now has a class in Richmond, North Yorkshire, as well as *ad hoc* teaching sessions at shows and exhibitions. She continues to run classes in rug-making and dyeing in her garden studio at home in Reeth.

Heather loves to teach and she really comes alive when she is passing on her enthusiasm to students of whatever age and ability. As she said, it is possible to create recognizable objects in hooky even if you cannot paint: after all, that is how she got started

Bolton Castle, mixed cuts, yarn and mixed fabrics on white linen, 2007. 32 x 24 inches (81 x 60cm). Collection of the artist

on faces (see Chapter 12, *The Reeth Parliament*). Teaching students with visual impairments in The Gambia is hard but very rewarding work, which Heather undertakes on an entirely voluntary basis through her social enterprise, Rug Aid cic.

Heather enjoys teaching mixed textures, especially when she can encourage her students to let their imaginations run riot in creating flowers. This beautifully balanced photo is richly endowed with flowers exactly where you need them in a rug, in the foreground. The big blue thistle-like flowers are globe artichokes. The delightful and typically English

herbaceous border running away on the right is part of the herb garden. As well as artichokes, it features the cheerful yellow-filled white faces of moon daisies and a couple of spikes of lavender very near the camera. The pink plant is soapwort, a plant with a long history and great variety of uses as a cleaning agent. The crushed leaves and roots have been used as soap since Renaissance times.

In front of the border is a narrow grassy path that runs alongside the top of a stone retaining wall around a rough patch of grass. The hurdles that surround this patch on the other side are apparently

The stone-built barn standing behind a dry stone wall.

The stones use a very wide variety of colors.

made by some of the Bolton Castle gardeners. In the middle distance is a classic stone-built dales barn. This has a narrow high slit window, which allows some air to circulate around the hay that was traditionally stored within the building.

Heather's version of the same view is a little simpler in some respects. She has reduced the complicated pattern of walls and fences to a minimum, and the retaining wall has become a line of stones on the ground, perhaps representing a broken-down wall. Although the complexity of the flower border has been reduced, the flowers themselves have not been simplified at all. Their splendidly bold colors and shapes are a marked contrast to the peace and order of the scene above and beyond the barn.

Heather made the artichokes using normal proddy and the other flowers with shaped proddy. In this simple technique, you cut the short proddy strip to whatever shape you need before using it; you can fold it in half and cut both ends the same if you wish, or cut each end separately.

The white petals are shaped proddy clumped around a yellow center made of hooked yarn. The mauve flowers are very simple to make: after cutting

Heather's beautiful proddy artichoke, with glitzy highlights and some yarn.

The purple flowers are made by an entirely different method to the white flowers.

a stack of petals to the desired shape, Heather tied a knot near the end of a narrow strip of yellow fabric and pulled it through the center of a petal from the front. She then pulled that strip back up through the center of another purple petal and tied it off, leaving each pair of flowers joined together by a short yellow strip. Adding a few green shaped proddy leaves around completed the scene.

The walls, too, are complex and rewarding to examine in detail. Heather has used an amazing range of colors to construct them, choosing and placing each color just as carefully as the men who built the actual walls chose the blocks of local stone from which they are built. These are dry stone walls, there is no mortar holding the blocks together, and they are a distinctive feature of the landscape of many parts of upland Britain. Heather chose her fabrics to include some bits of sparkle to simulate the way light reflects off the grains of quartz in the stone. In among the blocks on the ground, Heather has created tufts of tall grass using dyed yarn. She has fanned out the threads to form little clumps and they are very effective.

The landscape behind the barn is simpler in the rug than in real life — it could have looked messy at this scale if Heather had tried to include every detail. Knowing what to leave out is an important part of creating a pictorial rug. Making what you leave in tell the whole story, filling in the literal gaps, is an art Heather has perfected. Even in the simplified version of the landscape you get a very good feeling for the way the hills are rolling away into the distance. The varying intensity of their colors achieves that, with the most distant hill showing the dark shades produced by a dense covering of heather.

Above those hills, the hand-dyed flannel Heather has used creates an almost turbulent sky in which a large cloud is forming. This is an invention compared to the original photo, and I hope Gene will agree that it is an improvement. The sky in Gene's photo appears to be almost empty, and is typical of photos taken under the prevailing conditions, but is not necessarily atmospheric. Heather's random pattern in shades of blue is just right.

Heather adores making rugs that reflect the variety and richness of the area in which she lives. This rug is typical of her work in some ways (compare the tree to *Jackdaw Jeans* in Chapter 14, for instance) and unique in others (there is nothing even remotely like these artichokes in any other rug of Heather's), but it is clearly North Yorkshire in all its glory. Happily for Heather, the rugged landscape in which she is so happy to live lends itself perfectly to interpretation through the medium of rug-making. It also provides the perfect setting for teaching and learning the art of painting with fabric, as rug-making has been called.

Tussocks of grass made of yarn, the strands teased apart.

The sky above the distant hills.

Shaped petals, held in place in pairs by the yellow centers, with shaped proddy leaves.

18

Origins and Identity

A broadly smiling Heather lies on the beach at Roker, Sunderland.

A broadly smiling Heather lies outside a barn at Scarcote, North Yorkshire. *Archives of the artist.*

This rug illustrates selected highlights of Heather's life story in six panels. "It was difficult to do because when I first had the idea I simply didn't know how to plan it out," says Heather. "In the end I decided to tell the story clockwise from the bottom left, from the panel that shows me as a child to the one opposite which shows where I am today." Following her suggestion, that is how this chapter will relate the tales told by this fabulous rug. Wherever you start, you have the potential to unearth a rich wealth of family history and stories because this is one small part of a fascinating family tree laid out in a rug. The tree itself unites the panels, its sturdy trunk running up the center of the rug while its branches reach out right to its edges, enfolding each of the six fascinating and richly-detailed panels.

The first panel shows a smiling Heather, at about eight years old, lying on a sandy beach. She based this image of herself on a photo taken in a very different setting.

Heather has a charming photo, with a hint of double exposure in the bottom right, which shows her at the age of eight or so. It was taken at Scarcote, the farm where she spent many happy holidays as a child. Heather appears to be lying on some hay, possibly just outside a barn. Using every bit of artistic licence available to her, Heather has taken the jizz — the essence — of her young self and changed the setting to the sandy beach at Roker, just north of the River Wear in her home town of Sunderland. Many aspects of this story are expanded in the story of the rug *Scarcote* (see Chapter 8).

This first panel shows Heather as a happy child, her red hair catching the sun. Heather's confidence in her technique with large faces and hands was firmly established by the time she made this rug in 2007. This hard-won ability shows in the simple definition she brings to her own face by the palette of three colors she has used to create it. Her hands are clearly shown as they support that joyful head, already full of bright and creative ideas. Heather's home-knit cardigan is her mother's favorite color, blue. It does

Origins and Identity, mixed cuts and mixed fabrics on even-weave Scottish hessian, 2008. 38 x 31 inches (96 x 78cm). *Collection of the artist.*

The Roker Lighthouse, which stands at the end of Sunderland's harbor wall

not matter what color it actually was: this blue is perfect, reflecting the sky and the water and acting as a bridge between the red hair and pink skirt.

Heather has created shading and curves in the cardigan and skirt that follow the folds and shaping of the garments. These delineate her body beneath them as clearly as if they really were three-dimensional objects. Her legs, with feet clad in black shoes, are made using the same three shades as the other skin areas. It is worth looking again at the face and remembering Paul Valéry's instruction while doing so, "To see is to forget the name of the thing one sees", but it is impossible to forget that this is the juvenile version of the woman who created the rug — it is so clearly her.

Heather is lying on the sand that forms the beach between the harbor walls not far from Roker Lighthouse, which was built in 1903 at the end of the 2,880 feet (880m) long Roker Pier. At night, a newly-installed lens throws a beam of light up to 22 miles (35.4km) out to sea. Amazing new technology means that the single bulb that produces this life-saving beacon uses a meagre 70 watts of electricity an hour — the previous one consumed 1,600 watts.

The colors of the lighthouse, stripes of red and white, are mirrored in the colors worn by Sunderland Football Club. The team plays in the beautiful new Stadium of Light, very close to Roker. Heather may have overemphasized the intensity of the red and the brightness of the white, but her husband is a Sunderland Football Club supporter and those colors really matter to him! The stripes on their shirts are vertical, unlike those on the lighthouse, but Les likes to think that the team towers above their competitors just as the lighthouse towers over the entrance to the harbor.

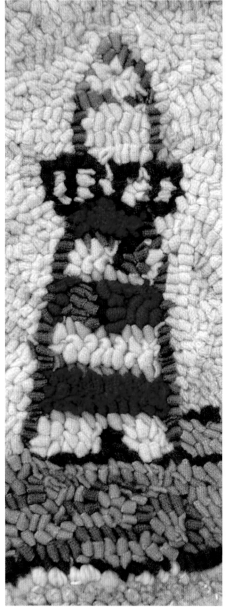

Heather's version of the lighthouse is only slightly romanticized.

The panel above Heather features a County Durham landmark, the Penshaw Monument. Heather said that this building was just as important to her mother as was the Fulwell Windmill near her father's allotment in north Sunderland (see Chapter 4, *Victory Garden*).

The Penshaw Monument was built in 1844 and is dedicated to John George Lambton. He was the first Earl of Durham and the first Governor of Canada. The monument appears on the coat of arms of Sunderland Football Club.

Heather says, "the Penshaw Monument uses lots of strong straight lines, and for that reason alone I hated doing it. I like doing higgledy-piggledy buildings. Irregular blocks of stone really lend themselves to hooking."

Despite this, Heather's use of greys and browns gives the monument a warmth and softness while keeping the definition of the structure clear. The huge red blossoms of poppies on the grassy slope in front of the monument enliven what could have been a stark image without them. It is well worth making the climb to the top of the hill to take in the wonderful views, but the monument itself is iconic rather than beautiful. As a landmark it is visible from miles around, and you know Sunderland is very near when you see it.

Looking across the Penshaw Monument you can see how the tree is wrapped around the panel, just as it encloses each of the others. Heather says, "I drew the tree, the tree of my life, to join parts of my history together. The pictures are fine hooky and the tree is cut and uncut high loops. I intended to add little animals and other figures in felting throughout the tree, like my dogs Fleet and Bonnie, the cats and the hens, but I haven't had the time."

The Penshaw Monument in the rug has slightly fewer columns than the real thing.

The Penshaw Monument – it's easy to see how Heather's simplification has improved it!

Looking across the Penshaw Monument, the tree's three-dimensionality is obvious.

Three different sections of the tree show the range of colors and textures it contains.

The ship is steaming toward the viewer – those are the anchor outlets (hawsepipes) near the prow.

All of the fabrics are wool, and in the tree Heather has used them mostly un-dyed. The tree shows only the long-lasting parts, the trunk and branches that hold it together, rather than the short-lived leaves. The only leaves in this rug form part of two panels: on a broad-leaved tree on the lower slopes of the hill supporting the Penshaw Monument and on a palm overhanging a beach in The Gambia. As with the buildings in *Reeth Village Green* (see Chapter 11), Heather introduces some unexpected colors into the wood: touches of red and pink and hints of blue and purple in the tweeds; she also uses a range of fabrics with different textures. You can tell that she has examined a tree; looking at something is easy, but really seeing it is a different experience.

The panel at the top left honors Heather's husband, Les, a retired Merchant Navy engineer. She says, "He helped me with the ship and especially the prow. He's okayed it, but you can't see him because he's in the ship's engine room where he worked. This panel is also a reminder of all my ancestors who worked in the shipping industry."

The quayside crane's hook hangs over the water.

The beautifully-formed sun is quite close to the water.

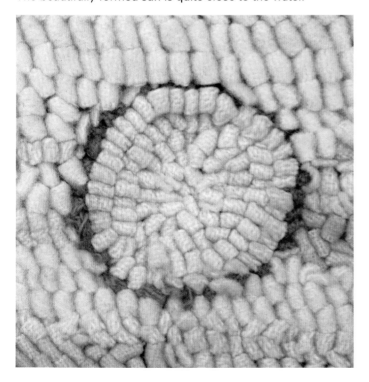

The sun is reflected on the water as this heavily-laden ship leaves the quayside. The crane in the background is a reminder of the busy time Les had at sea for most of his working life, performing maintenance tasks while the ship was in dock to make sure the engines were in tip-top condition and then keeping the engines running sweetly as the ship steamed its way around the world.

Heather says, "the colors in the sun's reflection are some of my favorites." Despite her claim not to have planned this rug, she says, "you have to think about color planning — it's a very important factor when you're making a rug. Values are important; you must have a contrast between dark and light colors. If it's all the same, it will be boring. You've got to think about the contrast between colors as much as the colors themselves."

She continues:

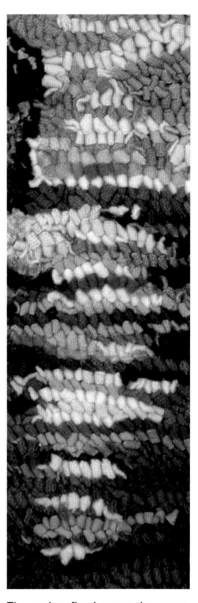

As well as the contrast, you must try to balance the colors. I felt I had too much blue in this rug, although I tried to marry some of the colors. I put a bit of purple at the top of the harbor sky because there was purple in the hills above Reeth. The yellow was the same — there was lots of yellow in the setting sun so I echoed it in the Gambian sand. I always try to marry and balance the colors because it's such an important factor.

When I'm doing a pictorial rug I think of telling a story. Your eye has to want to take a walk round the rug, to read the story. It has to be led through a picture so you have to think really carefully about the story you're telling

The sun's reflections on the water are disrupted by the ship's wake as well as the tide.

This keelman is clearly very proud of his fine uniform.

when you're putting pictures together like this. This rug is taking you into the past and back to the present and it's taking you all over the place too, from Sunderland to The Gambia via Swaledale.

The keelman, in the panel top right, represents Heather's great-great-grandfather, John Elliott. He plied his trade on the Wear, as is explained in Chapter 3, *The Ha'penny Ferry*. Here he is wearing his keelman's uniform.

This uniform is well-documented because the keelmen were an organized, almost unionized, group of workers. Every keelman wore a blue jacket over a yellow waistcoat with bell-bottom trousers and what is described as a blue bonnet. Heather's keelman is dressed ready for a hard day's work. He is standing on the prow of his keel and looks very proud, holding onto the lapel of his jacket. The level of detail in this panel is astonishing and it is almost possible to see how the green scarf around his neck has been tied.

Behind the keelman is Sunderland harbor. Heather has used artistic licence to recreate this busy part of the riverside as it might have been in Victorian times. It looks accurate and real, and these buildings use her palette of industrial colors to good effect. The buildings are very similar in color and shape to those she put behind her brothers in *The Evacuees* (Chapter 5).

The warehouses and dockyard buildings to the left of the keelman are tall, dark and well-defined, nearer than those on the right and with visible windows. Those to the right are shorter and less clearly-defined. They are also farther away across the water, distance which Heather has conveyed through the lighter colors she has used to build them.

The tall, dark-fronted warehouses nearest to the keelman

The more distant warehouses are less clearly defined, as is appropriate.

Behind the buildings on the right are what look like tall chimneys, possibly associated with some of the river-side industries of the Victorian era which required huge amounts of water, like paper- and glass-making.

The King's Arms' stone outer skin is clearly visible.

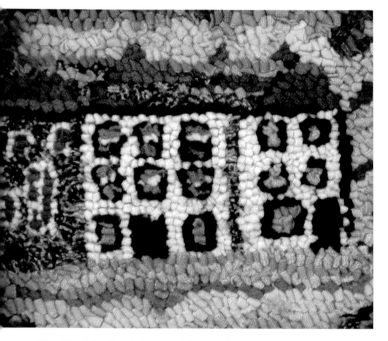

The Black Bull pub has a white render finish.

The Black Bull, The King's Arms and other High Row buildings, February 2010.

Below the keelman is a panel representing Reeth, where Heather now lives. This view shows the area known as High Row, with a stone-built private house on the left followed by the two pubs, The Black Bull and The King's Arms, either side of the alley that divides them. Finally three windows of Heather's one-time home, Overton House, peep over a branch of the tree on the right. The Black Bull has white-painted rendering over the rough stone blocks of which it is built, with dark keystone edges, and The King's Arms' stone is unpainted.

The grey ground immediately in front of the buildings is the cobbled area now used for parking. At one time they gave their name to a business operating out of Overton House, The Cobbles Tea Shop. The green for which Reeth is so famous lies nearest us, in front of the cobbles.

Heather and two students rug-making on a Gambian beach.

Heather with Jankey, one of the visually-impaired Rug Aid trainees. *Courtesy of Mat Connolley/Rug Aid cic*

Behind the row of buildings, the green lower slopes give way to the glorious purple shades of heather-covered Swaledale hills that rise high above the dale, all underneath a vivid August evening.

The panel at the bottom right is, in many ways, closest to Heather's heart. It shows her teaching rug-making in The Gambia with Rug Aid cic. The history of Rug Aid and a huge number of photos of Heather's work in The Gambia is available on www.rug-aid.org

The idea for this rug came from an exhibition Heather visited in Australia, called *Origins and Identity*. She says, "It was a wonderful exhibition and it inspired me. My origin is north east England and I identify myself as a teacher with this wonderful connection to Africa, hence this panel."

Rug Aid is a community interest company (cic) that Heather founded, with two supporters, in April 2007. It took over three years to convert an idea into a reality, but Heather has not looked back since Rug Aid cic came into existence.

Rug Aid runs rug-making workshops in Serekunda in premises loaned by the Gambian Organization for the Visually Impaired, GOVI. David Pointon, currently chairman of the UK organization that supports the school, The Friends of GOVI, lives in Wensleydale, just over the moor from Reeth. When Heather made contact with him, he and Pip Land welcomed her interest in working with blind people and helped Rug Aid to get the workshop running.

Heather first visited The Gambia in February 2007, returning in December that year. On each of those visits she was accompanied by her daughter Chrissie, who helped to assess the vision of potential students and provided some of them with glasses and magnifiers so that they could see their work. She also helped the Gambian rehabilitation officers and did some work with them. When Heather went back to The Gambia in March 2008, she trained ten women to act as teachers of rug-making and she has been back many times since then. Rug Aid's aim is that the workshops Heather sets up should become self-supporting, with rug-makers selling their own products to local people as well as to holiday makers. Rug Aid will teach the craft and, if possible, provide premises then step back to allow the workshop to develop as local conditions permit.

Because of my father, I have an interest in and sympathy with blind people everywhere. Begging, which most of the blind people in The Gambia used to rely on, has been banned and I felt driven to help them find another source of income. If I can pass on my knowledge of rug-making to help people with visual impairments in The Gambia to earn a living I will be very happy.

Showing Heather and two of her students working on rugs on the beach is artistic licence taken to its extreme. Heather works very hard to keep all the rugs out of the dust, which is in the air everywhere, and would never dream of taking them anywhere near the beach, although the ground upon which everyone walks and often sits is mostly rock-hard, bare earth. The rug-maker in the photo is working in her home compound in Serekunda, sitting on the ground and keeping her rug as clean as possible. Heather was very excited when she visited Mr. Musa's compound and saw this, because it showed her that rug-making is becoming an everyday activity, and that is the aim of Rug Aid's work. In the rug, each woman is hooking a strip of the same deep pink fabric; you can see the hook in the nearest woman's hand.

Heather has depicted herself wearing a warm fluffy jumper; it is way too hot for her to wear such a garment in The Gambia but it looks perfect in hooky. In a nice touch that brings the story told in this rug full circle, Heather's hair is the same color here as in the Roker Lighthouse panel.

Many Gambian women wear clothes made of printed cotton, brightly colored and richly patterned. The nearest woman is following Gambian style by wearing a head cloth which matches her dress.

This rug-maker is one of the sighted daughters of Mr. Musa, a visually-impaired director of the GOVI School. She is working on a rug in her home compound. *Courtesy of Heather Ritchie/Rug Aid cic*

Heather's fluffy pink jumper on a hot beach!

The only clear difference between Heather's hair is the sky, a pale Sunderland sky on the left and a vivid Gambian sky on the right.

The large palm tree is the only proddy in this rug. When the sky and the palm tree's trunk were both finished, Heather cut large leaf-shaped pieces of green fabric with pinking shears and prodded the long fronds into place. Heather also sewed the cowrie shells onto the beach when everything else was finished, and she gave the nearest woman an earring at the same time.

The palm tree that overhangs the Gambian beach.

A real earring hangs from a hooky ear.

Heather added some real cowrie shells to the hooky beach.

Choosing a title like "Origins and Identity" is bound to make you consider your strengths and weaknesses as well as your history. Heather says that she has great difficulty teaching rug-makers how to represent water, for instance, although she loves working on it herself. The water behind her in this panel is calm and beautiful, with the sunset reflected on the wave crests on the horizon and some tiny white waves breaking on the shore. The water in the panel opposite, within the harbour at Sunderland, is also beautifully depicted with its variety of colors and a suggestion of turbulence.

What all the panels have in common is a sky, but what different skies they are. The Gambian sky is dead straight rows of vibrant, sunset colors, and the Penshaw sky is dead straight rows of the palest blue. The keelman stands in front of a rich swirling sky, which suggests imminent rain, while the sky behind the lighthouse is a series of swirls of pale blue, echoing the pale blue water of the North Sea. The sky above Reeth is filled with sunset shades in shapes that echo the hills below it, and the ship is sailing out of a sky filled with pale shades of blue and yellow.

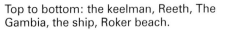

Top to bottom: the keelman, Reeth, The Gambia, the ship, Roker beach.

Naturally, the tree of Heather's life and history forms a border around the panel that depicts Heather's work through Rug Aid in The Gambia. This time, just as in the first panel, opposite, the roots of the tree are clearly visible below the panel. Heather has found a whole new set of roots in Rug Aid and its first project in The Friends of GOVI School. She hopes to replicate the success of that project in other deprived communities, giving Rug Aid roots in many places.

The tied-on label bears the one word, "Independence", to sum up what Rug Aid aims to give its trainees. *Courtesy of Mat Connolley/Rug Aid cic*

A view across the roots of the tree and Heather's work in The Gambia.

Glossary

allotment (garden): A plot of land, usually located alongside other such plots and rented from a local authority, on which fruit, vegetables and flowers are grown for personal consumption. Usually found in towns and cities to act as replacements for gardens.

Arkengarthdale: Valley running roughly north north west from Reeth.

as is: Using a textile in the color in which it was bought, whether that is natural or dyed.

backing: The open-weave fabric to which is attached the pile of a rug. Often made of jute (hessian/burlap) or linen.

bank: A bank is a small hill or other sloping land in north British English. In south British English the word refers to a riverside.

Beamish: A world-famous open air museum in County Durham that tells the story of the people of north east England. It holds an archive of rag rugs which the curator, Rosemary E. Allen, will open to groups by appointment.

bit: Regional name for rag rug, presumably derived from the fact that such rugs are made from bits of cloth.

bodgy: Regional name for rag rug: origin unknown.

bolt: A large roll of fabric.

Bolton Castle: Built between 1378 and 1399 by Richard le Scrope, Lord Chancellor, it is an example of a quadrangular castle whose component buildings are integral with the outside defensive walls that enclose a central courtyard, or quadrangle.

braces: Known as "suspenders" in the United States, where "braces" are found on teeth. In Britain, suspenders hold socks and stockings up.

bracken: Various species of large, coarse ferns which are commonly found on moorland.

broddy: Regional name for rag rug: origin unknown, possibly a derivation from "proddy".

burlap: Another name for hessian.

byre: A byre is strictly a cow-house, although the word is used more widely to mean a barn or outbuilding.

carding comb: Carding is the process of combing a bundle of fibers so that they end up oriented in the same direction. A carding comb is made of closely-spaced wire pins on a rubber backing: the shape, length, diameter and spacing of the wires varies between designs and applications. Heather's lap frame uses carding comb to hold the backing in place.

carpet tape: Also known as carpet binding, this is the strong cotton tape, about one and a half inches (3.5cm) wide, that Heather uses to cover the raw edges on the back of hooky rugs. Not to be confused with adhesive tapes, which are used to mend carpeting and/or stick carpets to the floor, it can also be used to secure a rug to a stretcher frame.

census: A count of people, as has been conducted in Great Britain every ten years since 1801 (except 1941). From 1841 onwards, the records provide valuable information about individuals.

chamber pot: Also known as a jerry or po, and made of pottery or metal. Before the advent of the indoor lavatory, a chamber pot would have been used in any room (or chamber) of the house to collect human waste.

chapel: In England, and particularly in Wales, a chapel is an independent or nonconformist place of worship.

charity shop: A thrift shop/store, hospice shop or op shop (from "opportunity shop"). A social enterprise: a retail establishment normally run by or on behalf of a charity for the purpose of fundraising, usually selling second-hand goods donated by members of the public and are often staffed by volunteers.

clapboard house: A style of architecture, common in New England, with horizontal boards on the outside of houses. Also known as bevel or lap siding and weather-boarding.

cleckie: Regional name for rag rug.

clippy: Regional name for rag rug, from the "clippings" used to make them.

clootie/clooty: Regional name for rag rug: from the Scots for "clothing".

collet: A collar around an object that exerts a strong clamping force when it is tightened via a tapered outer band.

community interest company (cic): An asset-locked limited company, one which cannot be sold for profit (in whole or in part) unless that profit is given to another asset-locked body or a charity.

community rug: A rug (historically most often a proddy mat) which is worked by a group of people. Often sold to raise funds for a good cause.

cree: A north of England word for the place where homing (or racing) pigeons are kept. It is called a loft or shed in other parts of the country.

crochet: Fabric created when loops of yarn are pulled through other loops. Heather's favoured technique for edging rugs.

Cushing Dyes: Fabric dyes made by W Cushing & Co., a company founded in Maine in 1879, which Joan and Bob Moshimer bought in 1968.

cut high loops: Loops of hooky that are pulled higher than those around them before having their tops cut off.

dale: A valley. Many dales, such as Swaledale, are named after the rivers that flow along the valley bottom.

Dales, The: The Yorkshire Dales National Park, although there are dales in Derbyshire as well.

directional hooking: Hooking that follows the direction suggested by the object being depicted rather than by the straight weave of the backing cloth.

dressmakers' net: Fairly stiff open fabric used to stiffen petticoats, can also be used to trace and transfer designs. Normally made of nylon, can be washed and re-used almost indefinitely.

dressmaking: The technique of making clothes using fabric (as opposed to knitting, crochet etc).

earth closet: Outdoor toilets, so-called because they were originally small rooms containing holes in the earth used to dispose of human waste (in contrast to the much later water closet).

Epsom salts: Magnesium sulphate, once a common domestic remedy, a laxative as well as a bath salt.

Fair Isle: An in-the-round knitting technique, which uses multiple colors to create patterns. Traditionally limited to five colors, with only two being used per row of knitting.

fantail pigeon: A pigeon whose fan-shaped tail contains 30 to 40 feathers. (Most members of the pigeon family have tails with 12 to 14 feathers.)

felt-tipped pen: A solvent-based pen used to draw on the hessian. The felt tip is essential to prevent damage to both pen and fabric.

fents: Remnants or offcuts of fabric, from a French word meaning "to split".

fitted carpets: Carpet that runs from wall to wall leaving no bare floorboards exposed.

flannel: A soft woven fabric that usually has no nap (raised surface) but gains its softness through the loosely spun yarn from which it is woven. It was originally made from carded wool or worsted yarn, but is now often made from either wool and cotton, or wool and synthetic fiber.

fleece: The coat of a sheep, usually removed by shearing and kept in one piece for ease of handling and processing.

flying end: The first or last part of a strip of hooky fabric, so-called because it does not form a loop. Should always be found in the same hole as another flying end, except at the outer edges of a piece of work.

Fremington Edge: Three miles (4.8km) of crags and scree slopes running north northwest and situated to the north of Reeth.

French knots: An embroidery technique in which the yarn or thread is knotted around itself.

Friends of GOVI, The: A registered UK charity founded in 1998, set up to support the only school for the blind in the Gambia where they work with and alongside GOVI, The Gambian Organization for the Visually Impaired.

Gambia, The: The smallest country in Africa, completely surrounded by Senegal. Its shape roughly mirrors the shape of the Gambia River, which flows into the Atlantic Ocean through the country's short western coastline. About one third of the population of 1.7 million people live below the international poverty line, on less than £0.80 (about US$1.25) a day.

glazing bars: The horizontal and vertical bars of wood or metal that separate a window into panes, each of which is filled with a glass panel.

GOVI: Gambian Organisation for the Visually Impaired, that runs a school in Serekunda.

grain: The lines of threads in fabric that give rise to its direction. With most fabrics used in rug-making, it is essential to cut along one of these directions to avoid shredding and disintegration.

guide dog: A specially-trained assistance dog for someone with a visual impairment.

ha'penny: A half penny (abbreviated to ha'penny after the common pronunciation of the word): there were twelve pennies (written "d") in a shilling (written "s") and twenty shillings in a pound (written "£") before Britain adopted decimal currency in 1971.

heather: Also called "ling", the most common plant in European heathland and moorland.

hessian: A coarse woven fabric usually made from jute, also known as burlap. Although she has used old sacks for rug-making both in the UK and The Gambia, Heather prefers to use only high-quality evenly-woven hessian, which is made in Scotland.

hook: The tool used to produce hooky rugs. Can be made of wood or of metal or a combination of both.

hooky: Rug-making technique that uses a strip of fabric about ¼ inch (6mm) wide and up to 14 inches (35.5cm) long. Common name for the resulting rag rug, from the tool used to make them.

hoop: A tool of two graduated wooden rings for holding fabric; a rug hoop differs from a tapestry hoop in that it has a much longer screw to cope with the greater thickness of fabric that lies between the rings.

hurdle: A moveable section of light fence, traditionally made from woven split branches (wattle) of hazel or willow.

ideas file: So that she has something to turn to when she needs a source for a particular subject, Heather files pictures she cuts out of magazines (and her own photos) of animals, flowers, buildings etc by type.

jackdaw: A bird, *Corvus monedula*, member of the crow family with dark plumage. The name first appears in the 16th century and probably comes from "Jack", meaning — in relation to animals — a small form, and the Old English word "daw", meaning "day" or "dawn".

jerry: Also spelled "gerri", another word for a chamber pot: possibly derived, during WWI, from "German".

jute: A soft, vegetable fiber whose strands are between one and four metres in length. Cloth woven from jute is called "hessian" or "burlap".

lap frame: Rigid wooden frame with some means of holding the hessian in place, possibly a spiky surface or lengths of overlapping wood.

lathe: A tool that spins a block of material (wood, metal) in order to shape it by cutting, sanding, drilling, etc.

light-fugitive: Any color that changes on exposure to light is said to be light-fugitive (literally meaning "fleeing from the light").

linen: A textile made from the fibers of the flax plant, *Linum usitatissimum*. Heather's preferred backing for rug-making.

Lisle: Lisle yarns have additional strength and resilience due to the presence of extra twists. The additional processing required means it is more expensive as well as more durable than basic cotton yarn.

list: Regional name for rag rug, from the Lancashire word for selvedge.

locker hooking: A technique for securing a section of un-spun fleece by working it around and over a length of yarn.

looped: Regional name for rag rug: from the shape of the pile.

monk's cloth: Named for the two threads that lie side-by-side on both the warp and the weft, 2x2 monk's cloth is soft and easy to use as a rug backing. Not to be confused with 4x4 monk's cloth that is more dense.

mood board: Similar to a scrapbook in content, a mood board is devoted to one project at a time and helps Heather to focus her thinking when working on a rug.

netty: Also spelled "nettie", north east England dialect for a lavatory in general and an earth closet in particular. Possibly derived from "necessity" or the Italian *gabinetti*.

Northern Echo, The: Daily newspaper published in Darlington since 1870.

patchwork: A branch of needlework that involves sewing pieces of fabric together to produce a pattern or design.

peggy: Regional name for rag rug, because rug-makers used one leg of a wooden clothes peg.

permanent marker: Solvent-based, felt-tipped pen used for drawing a design on the backing and recording details about the rug on the carpet tape on the reverse.

piece: Regional name for rag rug: from the "pieces" of fabric.

pigeon cree: North eastern name for a pigeon loft or dovecote, used to house racing pigeons.

pile: The part of a rug that is attached to the backing.

po: Another word for chamber pot, possibly derived from the French word "*pot*" and pronounced without the final "t".

poked: Regional name for rag rug, from the poking technique used.

pricked rug: Regional name for rag rug: from pricking through the backing.

prodder: The tool used to produce proddy rugs. Blunt-ended and made from wood or metal or a combination of the two.

proddy: Rug-making technique that uses short strips of fabric, up to three inches (7.6cm) long and ½ inch (12mm) wide. Widely-used name for the resulting rag rug.

proggy: Regional name for rag rug: from a mispronunciation of "proddy" maybe?

rag: Regional name for rag rug, from the type of fabrics used.

Received Pronunciation: Sometimes called the Queen's (or King's) or BBC English, accent-free English is not superior to regional versions of the spoken language.

recycled fabric: Fabric that is not undergoing its first use, such as second-hand clothes and worn-out blankets.

rehabilitation officer for people with visual impairments: Someone who helps people with limited eyesight to understand what tools and equipment are the most appropriate for their needs and teaches their use.

remnant: The fabric that remains at the end of a bolt.

reverse proddy: A technique that results in a series of overlapping "stitches" of fabric on the front and (short) loops on the back of a rug.

River Tyne: The North and South Tyne rivers meet near Hexham in Northumberland and flow to meet the North Sea at Newcastle.

River Wear: Rises in the Pennine hills and flows east through the City of Durham to meet the North Sea at Sunderland.

Roker: Part of the city of Sunderland, north of the River Wear and on the coast, once the home of Sunderland Football Club.

Roker Lighthouse: The lighthouse stands at the end of Roker Pier (which is 2,880 feet [880m] long) at the place where the River Wear meets the North Sea.

rotary cutter: A hand-cranked device for cutting strips of fabric for hooky work, or a hand-held cutting tool with a circular blade. The former can cut several strips at once, from fine to quite wide.

Rug Aid cic: Social enterprise founded by Heather in 2007 to teach rug-making in The Gambia, www.rug-aid.org

sale of work: A fund-raising sale at which handicrafts are sold to raise money for a cause, the items usually made by members of the community that benefits from the sale, as was the case with the Methodist Ladies of Arkengarthdale and their proddy rug.

scrapbook: A large format book of blank pages onto which are glued pictures from magazines, pressed flowers, snatches of poetry, scraps of fabric that catch the eye and the imagination.

shaggy: Regional name for rag rug: from the shaggy appearance of the rug.

shaped proddy: A hooking technique for flowers and leaves. In one method (see the palm tree in *Origins and Identity*, Chapter 18) fabric is cut to shape before prodding it through the backing. In the other method (see the Christmas roses in *Bearing Gifts* in Chapter 14), a length of yarn is tied in a knot at one end. Using a needle or bodkin, the yarn is pushed through the center of one shaped proddy strip, brought to the front and through another strip, and is tied off.

sneck: Part of the latch of a door, the lever that raises the bar that keeps the door shut. It has a thumb plate on one side that you press down and a short bar on the other side that you lift: both actions raise the bar and open the door. Moving this lever makes a distinct metallic sound.

soft furnishings: Curtains and cushions etc. used as decorative features in interior design.

stobby: Regional name for rag rug: from the Northumberland word for "stubble".

stretcher frame: Wooden frame used for rug-making characterized by short "stretchers" pegged to keep the long sides apart, thereby keeping the backing taut. Can be large, enabling up to 10 people to work at once.

Sunderland Echo: Evening newspaper published in Sunderland since 1873.

Swaledale sheep: Sheep with black faces, sometimes marked with white; both males and females grow curled horns. Their coats are thick, straight, coarse and of a uniform white color and their wool is durable and resilient.

sweater: Heavy- and light-weight knitted garments.

tabbie: Regional name for rag rug: from "tabs," bits of waste fabric.

tabby cat: An astonishingly wide variety of colors and coat patterns lurk under the five letter word "tabby." Heather's cat Timmy was a classic Mackerel tabby.

tapestry hoop: A pair of wooden hoops, a smaller one of fixed size and a larger one with an adjustable screw fixing, which fit together. Fabric for needle (or hooky) work is held taut between the two. A hooky frame has a longer screw to permit a greater thickness of fabric to be held still.

tatty: Regional name for rag rug: origin unknown.

thrum: Warp threads, up to nine inches (22.8cm) long, which were left on the loom when the finished piece of cloth was cut off. Mill workers were allowed to take the pieces of yarn home for rug-making.

tweed: A rough woollen fabric, coarse and unfinished with a soft, open texture. It is made in either plain or twill weave and may have a check or herringbone pattern. Sometimes made by twisting differently colored woollen strands into two- or three-ply yarns, which results in interesting "heather mixture" color effects.

upland: In the Yorkshire Dales, dry heaths dominated by heather.

vanishing point: The point in a perspective drawing at which parallel lines appear to converge.

Waldoboro: A sculpted (sheared and shaped) style of rug-making that started in the fishing community of Waldoboro, Maine.

warp: The threads that are attached to a loom, through which the weft is threaded. Warp threads must be strong to withstand the tension put on them.

weft: Also called "woof," the threads that are woven through the warp on a loom. Weft threads can be less strong than warp threads. The word comes from the Old English word "wefan" meaning "to weave".

Index